DROPS OF WATER,
GRAINS OF SAND

---

by

James C. Courtney

TRAFFORD

Printed in Victoria, Canada

Note for Librarians: a cataloguing record for this book that includes Dewey Classification and US Library of Congress numbers is available from the National Library of Canada. The complete cataloguing record can be obtained from the National Library's online database at: www.nlc-bnc.ca/amicus/index-e.html

ISBN 1-4120-1699-1

This book was published *on-demand* in cooperation with Trafford Publishing.
On-demand publishing is a unique process and service of making a book available for retail sale to the public taking advantage of on-demand manufacturing and Internet marketing. **On-demand publishing** includes promotions, retail sales, manufacturing, order fulfilment, accounting and collecting royalties on behalf of the author.

Suite 6E, 2333 Government St., Victoria, B.C. V8T 4P4, CANADA

Phone	250-383-6864	Toll-free	1-888-232-4444 (Canada & US)
Fax	250-383-6804	E-mail	sales@trafford.com
Web site	www.trafford.com	TRAFFORD PUBLISHING IS A DIVISION OF TRAFFORD HOLDINGS LTD.
Trafford Catalogue #03-2076		www.trafford.com/robots/03-2076.html	

10   9   8   7   6

DEDICATION

To my beloved grandchildren:

Megan, Daniel, Anna, Emilee and Makenzie

To Jack Wilson —
Thanks for your many
kindnesses over the years —

Jim Courtney

PREFACE

Over time a man thinks many things: he writes down very few. As I approach my allotted "three score and ten" I am trying now to remember thoughts of the past. I want to write down that which I am about to forget. I have no answers to life nor any advice. Life is a riddle to me. Yet there are clues. They are to be found in what we think when our minds are allowed to set aside the tedious aspects of living: bank account, appointments, obligation, business objectives, etc. The kind of thinking to which I allude is a sort of recreation of the mind. Not relaxation so much as active exercises of the brain. As the body may use sports to recreate, so the active mind needs flexing, more often than we imagine, and this is what I do as I write.

Mine is merely a process of remembering my childhood, youth, adulthood, aging and possible onset of dotage. It is "The Ages of Man" minus everybody else. It is about me. After all, isn't that what my life is all about? Me? What is your life all about? Perhaps we think alike on many matters. Maybe we even disagree on certain matters. (I can say truthfully that I do not always agree with what I say or write. Also, sometimes I exaggerate and even lie.) I do not teach. We all constantly struggle to learn.

For a time I felt like a stranger in this world. Later an overnight guest. Then a combatant striving to survive. In my fifties I became somewhat disentangled from the "struggle" of life. I relaxed and had some real fun. More comfortable with myself and feeling somewhat apart from others but still at one with the process of living, I began to relax. More importantly, feeling more at peace with myself, I began to live. I should have learned about living much earlier.

That same, slow process of adjustment has occurred with my writing. Somehow it has become easier for me. Perhaps my editors will feel that it seems easy to me because it lacks quality. I am writing what I feel in the best way I can. What else might I do? Write for the editors? I write my thoughts for myself and for my welcome companions, the greenhorns and the grizzled, the young and old, as we proceed on our strange, wonderful voyage of life.

> *I do not seek agreement with all that I may write.*
> *Tolerance is the most that a penman can ask.*
> *I'll elucidate with honesty and avoid being trite.*
> *I will hide behind no pen name, shield or mask.*
> (Anon.)

James C. Courtney 2003

DROPS OF WATER
GRAINS OF SAND

An expedition to a strange land can alter one profoundly. By traveling outward we discover more of the landscape of our inner nature.

***

Hold your children tightly. Yet they will grow; out of your arms, out of your home, away from your care, into their own place where they will have children who will someday wave goodbye, leaving your children behind.

***

What is an old man to do? His decrepitude masks his long ago, youthful, bountiful adventures of discovery. Even his language seems antiquated. The young rush by in search of knowledge and the dust from their shoes settles in the gray hair of their lonely, would-be teacher.

***

Being a parent is a responsibility. Being a grandparent is a delight. Love minus Responsibility equals Bliss.

***

We all pay for romantic love. The process of enchantment, exuberance, commitment, responsibility, disappointments, and death, Yet all these combined are not too high a price to pay.

***

We all know black, white and red. But few things are so sublime as black trees against a white sky and a black squirrel foraging in the white snow while a bright, crimson cardinal passively observes from atop a snow-capped, gray fence post. The sight makes pretty Christmas cards.

***

All our lives we search for a second mother; an emulator. It is a lucky man who finds her. Do not despair. Perhaps she is even now browsing through life, looking for you. To find her you must get up, go out and wander.

***

The new snow clings to the bare branches. We all know that it will finally fall like the lately descending leaves. The snow will slowly melt and drip, or a cruel wind will suddenly sweep it to the ground. Yet it clings, it grips, it hangs on up there. Empathizing, we watch and hope for one more day.

***

Live today. Use it up. "Someday, today will be a very long time ago." (*anon.*).

***

There is no such thing as a just punishment. It is either too harsh or too lenient. Only in retrospect can we judge the judgment. Then it's too late.

***

It's not your being dead that hurts so much; its your being gone, I think. I have recovered from the shock of your death but I can't get over your absence.

***

When first we love, we speak of fantasy and forever. Later we select our language with more care, as though to forget our youth. The passage of time may alter our ardor. Whisper or holler, "I love you", to the one across the table.

***

redundant: reiterating again something superfluous which has already been restated before.

***

Why is it that rich uncles live forever while penniless fathers die so young?

***

It would be delightful to have in one's purse so much money that when he has wasted a night in eating, drinking and other merriment he might regret only the time allotted thereto.

***

Upon the sudden death of an extremely corpulent friend it was said at his wake that he "ate not wisely but too well".

***

As he grew older he became even more vain. The degree of his vanity was best expressed by his total lack of attention to his personal appearance.

***

Upon viewing the dozen or so photographs placed upon my mother's grand piano, depicting her children, nieces, nephews, grandchildren and great-grandchildren, I was moved to comment, "Oh what a tangled web we weave when first we fashion to conceive".

***

Jokes are almost always very serious metaphors for life.

***

He had the ability to become intriguingly evasive.

* * *

Nobody ever made any money by leaving things alone.

* * *

I refuse to become a rung on somebody else's ladder. I try, each day, to become another step on my own ladder.

* * *

It seems strange that envy often generates a hatred rather than admiration. And a desire to emulate, ever falling short, often turns to envy.

* * *

When things go wrong we beg God's help. When things work well we take all the credit. God is patient with us in this matter.

* * *

While we relax and enjoy a leisurely dinner, chat with out hosts, sip our wine and savor a cigar, a goose flies the Mediterranean from Valencia to Algiers.

* * *

To marry is finally to relinquish the general in favor of the particular.

* * *

Hunger sharpens the mind. Food dulls us for a time, till, in due course, elemental cravings begin to recur and all is well again.

* * *

Brother or sister is, by turns, competitor, companion, defender and friend.

Father is stranger, provider, demigod, teacher, judge, then finally confidant.

But mother is always mother.

* * *

If you play a musical instrument, play it well. Otherwise play it in the shower.

* * *

Of course women are vastly different from men. Otherwise what is the point?

* * *

When a man sees the woman he would marry he knows it almost immediately. He will take longer to select an automobile than he will to choose a lifelong mate. Impulse triumphs over reason. The eyes have it.

***

To psychoanalyze one's self is to enter into a house of mirrors with mere candlelight. You will not recognize the truth if you see it, and when reaching out confidently to grasp at an image, it will surely shift into its opposite.

***

Pity for the man who collects many things. He is seeking to find himself in his possessions and failing in that, ever deluded, lost among his belongings, he will simply collect more things. Ultimately, when the undertaker and the auctioneer have concluded their work, there is left but a shroud, a casket, a plot and a stone. Who was this man? Did anyone really know him?

***

Owning an ample and diverse library can have positive consequences. Seeing all the books, guests will be impressed and expect you to posses great knowledge and even wisdom. Realizing this, and desiring to maintain the respect of your admirers, you may very well take up reading.

***

An actor is the biographer of his on-stage character. If he does his job well you will leave the theater certain that you now know the character. But the actor? Alas; absolutely no one knows the actor.

***

If you would be literate then keep a dictionary nearby. Read one page a day and avoid newspapers and novels. There is more knowledge, mental exercise and pure joy obtained from learning new words than there is in the whole of a university education.

***

If God loves us so much then why didn't he make us out of titanium?

***

My dictionary says: "**trite**: *worn out by constant repetition*." Therefore it follows that most trite comments are probably true, but nobody really listens anymore.

***

There are many items on my "wish" list. Living forever is not among them.

***

I am sad when I see people my age searching out the old, popular songs; music from their youth. As if by replaying the music they might recapture a portion of their lives which, in reality, was not so wonderful as recalled; nor was the music. Acknowledge yesterday as history, function well today and hope and plan for tomorrow. Like it or not, to survive man must be contemporary.

**

The Perpetual Triumvirate: The Owners of Production have the wealth, The Politicians legislate and administer the laws by permission of and in cooperation with their affluent sponsors and The Church, which promises us a better life after we die, provided we submit to and obey current laws while we live. They tell us to "Render unto Caesar, etc." These three Masters, working closely together, rule all. One cannot imagine another world.

**

When a man reaches the state of maturity, usually in his forties, his view of the world is nearly always complete and static. Do no try to teach this man, nor change his habits, his politics or religion or his outlook on the world. If you desire his friendship you must exercise tolerance and/or feign agreement. Life is too short and friends too scarce to waste a moment in fruitless bickering.

**

It is in Man's nature always to be searching. So we explore the boundless jungles, cure diseases old and new, split the atom, build larger telescopes, go to the Moon and grasp for the Stars, . Then further out we go, into the boundless universe of the subconscious, human mind, where dwell love, hate, hope and fear: where live angels, harpies, dragons, unicorns and dreams.

**

A first class nation which treats its teachers as second class citizens will presently become a third rate society.

**

To judge another person by a peculiar accent or by the color of his skin, is to be both deaf and blind. Accept the small variances of others. Withhold judgment. Open your mind. Yet tolerance is not enough. For a society to function successfully, there must be the capacity for love.

**

In the simultaneous duties of father, son, brother, husband, provider and friend, a man must strive to perform life as if to play all six strings of a guitar. When executed with practiced skill and devotion, the many complex harmonies thus produced can be almost ethereal. The audience is thrilled.

***

Playing solitaire is a waste of time. But so is listening to music, viewing a sunset, reading a novel, mowing a lawn and taking a leisurely bath . There is more to life than working to make the world a better place and failing in the attempt. Solitaire sharpens the brain and gives the conscience a rest. Deal.

***

I have seen men brought low by liquor, drugs, tobacco smoking and even overwork, but nothing is so sad as watching the ruination of a man as he pursues a woman who does not want to be caught.

***

One can reread a book, play a recording repeatedly, look at old photographs, recite a remembered poem and tell stories of the past. But man cannot relive one second of his life, turn back one page, or amend a thoughtless word. Regret can be addressed with an apology and a promise never to repeat the injury. One can confess sins and be forgiven. Yet one can never go back and undo. Therefore take care in your actions and your words. Remorse is peculiarly agonizing because it is always freshly painful and forever too late.

***

Never trust a woman with three colors of hair.

***

Heroism and cowardice exist together inside each of us. They both may express themselves in situations and at times unexpectedly. No person knows for certain which he will become until events conspire to reveal his response.

***

The difference between the stock market and a casino is that the former uses computers and brokers while the latter uses money chips, dealers and pit bosses. Both offer us hope, fear and more than a taste of greed. Both are as habit-forming as narcotics and both have been legal, in one form or another, since long before the money changers bargained at the Temple and the Roman soldiers cast lots beneath the Cross of Jesus.

***

A man must live with his mistakes. He must regret acts omitted and repent for sins committed; but he must survive. Therefore he must endeavor to make every day a day of expiation. He must redress all his wrongs as best he can. He must work to improve himself and the small world he inhabits. This is all he can do. Man does not die for his sins; he survives within a life of atonement.

***

Seek physical recreation through games. Games train the body and the mind. They nurture the will to excel. They teach young people to compete; to interact with others within the rudiments of physics, mathematics and nature. They teach the dynamic of fellowship and the complex duality of winning and losing. They train one for the confrontations in the game of life. They coax the mature person to remain young by flexing old muscles. Play games.

***

Anatomy and temperament dictate that a woman excel in tactics while a man devise strategies. She acts from instinct while he is motivated by vision. She is his dream and he is her willing instrument. Together they can make a family.

***

Why is it that God, in almost all religions, is accepted as a Man; a "He"? Woman maintains a secondary rank. Yet kings, conquerors, gods and prophets; all men come from Woman. Muhammad and Jesus both had mothers who nursed and nurtured them. The mystery of Man and Woman is older than all the gods. Hidden within the mystery is the magic.

***

Information without intelligence is simply cold fact. Intelligence without data is but inert potential. Depending upon the quality of both, a mind, combining these two, may give birth to awesome inventions; both constructive and destructive: the wheel, the steam engine, the hula hoop and the neutron bomb.

***

The most precious aspect of a democracy is that, within the limits of accepted laws, each citizen has the unalienable right to behave foolishly.

***

In life, nothing makes sense. Everything ends badly. That's why we concoct fiction, erasers and absolution.

**

A playwright disguises truth in the form of a fantasy. That fiction is then turned back into a sort of truth by the actor. The actor possesses the power to bring forth the truth hidden inside this fantasy. The actor, then, is a crafty magician changing a silk scarf into a flying white dove. Applauding his skill, we recognize that the dove was indeed in there, inside the script, all the time.

**

Life is short. We are born, we live, we die; some soon, some late. Before you appeared there was a near infinity of time. Now that you have luckily arrived, do not forget to live. Life is short. Death is forever.

**

People change. Friends experience alterations in their lives, their habits, their likes and dislikes. Today's friend is apt to become tomorrow's mere associate. You will change also but, even so, you are always you. Therefore, take care and so act, as to remain your own, loyal, nurturing, best friend.

**

Life is a series of wins and losses. A man can learn to live with that fact and enjoy the game. But if, in any way, he cheats at the venture, though he may appear cheerful in his manner, he is remorseful. Though he smiles, he is in pain. His deceitfulness has metastasized. His world collapses. Playing by the rules is safer and more fun. It makes both living and dying easier.

**

Most people would not want to live life over. The wise say, "Once is enough". But all this is forgotten when we watch a laughing child taking his first steps.

**

The more our thoughts dwell upon the glory that was yesterday, steeped in reveries, the sooner we will become a permanent captive of the past.

**

Life is regulated by a gigantic, numbered wheel. Every morning we awake from our dreams to play the game, trying to stay in the game. Day upon year we play. There is but one certainty of the game: the house finally wins.

**

Pursue your objectives now. Do not wait until another day. Deferred hopes and delayed actions quickly spoil and become a drooping bouquet of yesterday's neglected dreams. Do it today.

***

Listen to the signals in the music; the call to battle and the beckoning to love, the barroom ballad and the children's nonsense song, the symphony and the campfire melody. Music plucks at heart strings. Music speaks to the milestones of our lives. From the first lullaby we hear but do not remember, to the dirge played at our funeral, which we know well but do not hear.

***

Life is comprised of elements of both fantasy and reality. These are always blended. A prudent man combines these two volatile elements with great care and knows full well which is which. But woe to him who gets the two confused.

***

Once I had both a wife and a mistress. Looking back now, through the gray screen of time, it was as if I were in a jail cell and slipped away periodically to be tortured on the rack, and I did it all with a smile. And I paid all the bills.

***

I knew the moment I saw her that I wanted her, I would possess her, marry her and share my life and fortune with her. I knew too that my old, selfish hopes and dreams must be deferred and that I was lost to myself forever.

***

Romantic love is simply nature's way of populating the planet. Love is exciting and fun and an excellent bonding device between a man and a woman. It seems to work well. Love can cement a relationship and thus provide a bit of stability for the children as they grow. Otherwise how would children come to be nurtured? Romantic love is a timing device, set to detonate simultaneously in two ripened people. Love is a perfumed breeze beneath a shady willow.

***

The high esteem in which man holds himself is disgraceful. We feel we are somehow better than "animals". For to admit that the past and future of man is nothing special, nothing "better" is to devalue our own species. As if claiming that rape, murder, torture, war and the destruction of our own heaven-on-esarth somehow places us in the pantheon of the gods. Man's history and man's own, current, repeated follies are sufficient cause to de-humanize him. Who among us has not sometimes wished he were a lion or an eagle?

***

One cannot make a book from a life nor a ballet from a poem, nor can we shape a song from a crystal, trilling brook. Nor is a painting of a woman ever the woman. Yet we keep trying. What we do create sometimes has its own peculiar, appealing quality. Only man can create fantasy. Never fear to create.

***

Evolution, as described by Darwin, is decried by the Churches. Yet does anyone truly believe that God would create such a predator as man? Man kills his own kind in war, in rage, in envy and jealousy. He kills for food when his larder is already full. He kills other species for amusement. Man is a disgrace. There is either God or there is Man. We can fully comprehend neither.

***

When I was twenty years old, the woman, for whom I would happily have given my life, married another. She is old now and so am I. I would not give her a second glance today, nor would she I, except that once we loved each other.

***

A man of advanced years often foolishly seeks a younger woman. He plans to plunder her youth and thereby make of it his own. Soon she will make him feel even older. He may attempt this folly again and again. Each woman will soon find herself a more suitable mate. Be content, old man. Leave the chase to the fleet. Are you really prepared for repeated failure, humiliation and defeat?

***

There are rules of religious dogma, common law, custom, etiquette, tradition, and of the community. There are rules to tell us how we may act, what we may view, what we may say and even, at times, what we may think. The purveyors of these conventions always lose in the end and finally they are passed by; encompassed by those ever constricting walls; lonely, expiring prisoners, inside their self-made, crumbling fortress. A man can die of too many rules.

***

Liquor is the enemy of the priest, the teacher, the writer, the broker, the doctor, the pilot, the farmer and the merchant; that is unless the merchant sells liquor.

***

"Blasphemy" is a word invented by clergy to keep the flock in order, to prevent unorthodox thought from verbal expression and discourage straying from prescribed dogma. As a sheep dog herds by instinct, the clergy vigilantly strives to direct our action, thoughts and words. The Border Collie and the clergyman each labors unremittingly, keeping his flock ever in order.

***

The beauty of suicide is that it may always be deferred till tomorrow. It is the portal through which we may pass at our time of choosing to escape the terrors and pains of today at the cost of all hope for tomorrow. The sad part is that it can be done only once and is irreversible. Better hope for a better tomorrow.

***

If wishes were horses, fodder would trade as a prized commodity while saddle makers and stable-hands would rule the world.

***

The man who wants to live forever misses the point of life. Life, like gold, is precious only because it is finite. It is important to the living only because we know that we will die. Death is a small price to pay for the billions upon billions of odds against our ever having been born. It is the rarity and brevity of life which gives it value. From eternity to eternity, each living thing is allowed a tiny taste of existence. Therefore be grateful for life and neither fear nor mourn your death. That last emotion belongs entirely to your survivors.

***

There are no perfect mothers and no perfect fathers. There are no perfect children. Perfection is a thought in the mind of God. We live in a flawed world where the just ever strive toward that attainment. We often slip and fall, but regain our legs and continue the mission. All ultimately die and we who survive justly give them praise. We each continue, hoping to give our brief lives some significant meaning.

***

Acquittal may be rendered by a jury. Absolution might be given by a priest. Apologies may be provisionally accepted or even rejected. For total, complete forgiveness we must look to God. Only then can we begin to forgive ourselves.

Perhaps the curse of Man was not of: "The knowledge of good and evil", but the knowledge of his own mortality. Only Man contemplates his own death.

***

A necessary component of joy is surprise. Happiness may last even a lifetime but joy is ephemeral. The first snows of winter bring joy to the viewer but to be happy one must learn to thrive in all seasons and every climate.

***

As a rule, people believe in God because they cannot imagine an alternative. Imaginative people live in a world of many doubts. Through their creativity in the arts and sciences they will seek, and they too will gain, their salvation.

***

It is best to have brothers and sisters. Being an only child is too heavy a burden to bear. Therefore do not grumble at dividing an inheritance.

***

Your son will not be a copy of you. He is a new person. He is original. Treasure his uniqueness. Nurture his individuality. Teach him well so that someday he may validate and enlighten you through his originality.

***

A prodigal son is always welcomed home. An unruly daughter may return to the love and understanding of her parents. But where does a feckless father go to find a warm fire and a gentle touch?

***

"atrophy" v.& n. "waste away through under-nourishment, aging or lack of use; to become emaciated". That definition reminds me of my youthful hopes, dreams and promises and the careless manner in which I misplaced them.

***

Maintain a good relationship with your first wife. You may need her memory when it comes time to write your autobiography. But seek a second opinion.

***

The sun rises. All night I have watched as the distant city lights bounce off the cloudy sky and tumble down upon the stark white snow that covers all. Now and then the moonlight sneaks through the clouds and there is a further burst of brightness. I have seen deer in my yard tonight and a dozen raccoons and a white owl watching along with me. Now the squirrels appear, down from their nests, and are digging into the snow for one more acorn. I wonder what I shall do today. Perhaps I will follow the snowy owl to sleep.

***

It is asserted by some that "all men are created equal". This is not so. In all known species there is an order of dominance. Wolves, deer, lions, squirrels, apes, chickens, etc. all have their pecking order. Men are created equal in the eyes of God, perhaps, but mankind soon mercilessly sorts them out; often even before they are born. We live in the jungle and survive by its laws. All that can be truly said is that all men are created equally.

***

When one innocent man is punished or one guilty man is acquitted the judicial system is wounded. But when capital punishment is allowed, an error, if discovered too late, can deal a death blow to the society. Therefore take care, black robed jurist; the life of Justice rests in your hands.

***

Lawyers' tricks and lawyer jokes are older than those told of Portia and Shylock. They are as old as the profession to which lawyers have sworn allegiance. Lawyers perform a necessary function in any society, as do doctors, veterinarians, chemists, warriors, garbage collectors and politicians. It is only when all the politicians are lawyers and they make the laws that favor litigation and lawyers become involved in almost every dispute, be it petty or grand, civil or criminal; it is then that the jokes take on a darker complexion. Would we ever design a legislature where all the members were of any single profession?

***

Men die of a variety of diseases but the warrior dies from a disease in the minds of his leaders. This disease is called hubris and its young victims are but proxies. Leaders die abed in their eighties.

***

And God created the world and all things in the world and saw that is was good. Next, He decided that the world needed fables and myths, comedy and tragedy. So He sprinkled the world with millions of enigmas: Mankind.

Both laws and common sense acknowledge that sins can be ranked according to their seriousness. There is grand and petty theft. There is murder and manslaughter; and so on. Very high on the list of crimes are those committed by public servants in whom we place our trust and security, along with the ministers of faith to whom we entrust our souls. The greatest tragedy occurs when these honored few, being discovered to be criminals, go unpunished.

***

If you are ever subjected to the rage of one who is "blowing off steam", be calm. Be certain that all the steam is gone and the container has begun to cool before you utter a word. Save yourself from a scalding.

***

The best of poems and music may seem ambiguous to many listeners. Therefore use poems only as a composer uses music: to express emotions. If others find the tones appropriately pleasant or sad then you have, as a secondary result, communicated. But if your sole aim is to communicate, then use prose. The world thinks in prose. It dreams in music and poetry.

***

When a man of advanced years meets the woman of his dreams she is sure to be a product of a dream of long ago; when he was young. So she will be young. He should be complementary, polite, and soon move away: escape. For if, by chance, his dream should become a reality he will soon be living a nightmare. Dreams of lusty passion, when fulfilled, are the life affirming, driving force of the young and the agonizing torment of the aged.

***

A preacher may strive and even give his life to save men's souls in some far-off land, yet turn a blind eye to the extinction of one or more of God's "lesser", other creatures. God made us all. May He, therefore, protects us all.

***

The most desirable woman you will ever meet is your personal Venus Fly Trap. If you are not very lucky, she will devour you. It is her nature to consume you and yours to be consumed. Choose your predator with care.

***

If a man were somehow to possess every woman he ever desired he would be dead at twenty, or sooner, not from a shot fired by a jealous husband but by exhaustion. Man does not always know what is good for him.

***

Never write a word that you would be embarrassed to see quoted on the front page of the Sunday newspaper. "The written word remains." (*anon.*)

***

In my youth I experienced great pain and inexpressible joy in school. Algebra was hell and geometry was heaven. The library was 'Pleasure Island" and the gymnasium was a torture chamber. My chums were alter egos for me and the girls were unattainable desires. Yet, somehow, I became an educated adult even as I was staunchly resistant at every step.

***

To believe in The Bible and act on its precepts is to undertake a long trip on a winding road with detours and cutbacks; with the length of the trip uncertain and the destination more than somewhat obscure. The map is fragmented and pieces are missing. Absolute Faith is difficult to retain.

***

If a determined man were to *prove* to me that there is God, he will have robbed me of faith. For faith consists of believing in something which cannot be proved. Prove it and faith is no longer required. It evaporates. Some men wander the world, looking for Noah's Ark or The True Cross. They strive to prove every aspect of The Bible. Be careful, lest you steal our faith. "**faith** n. **1** complete trust or confidence. **2** firm belief, esp. without logical proof".

***

Mother and Father build his crib. Then they help select his playthings and send him to a school. As a grown man, he builds his own house, and, in time, selects his coffin. Of all these things, the crib deserves the most attention.

***

I am an older man preparing for a visit from a beautiful, younger woman. Something may happen tonight. I shower, shave, choose a cologne, select my clothes with care, study myself in the mirror. I arrange recorded dinner music. I await the doorbell. My palms sweat. I am a shy teenager.

***

A man's personal history must be viewed as a representative speck, or pixel, on the portrait of Man. A virtual eternity preceded him and, to an extent, holds him captive. Man is the sum of his life plus the lives of millions of generations of predecessors. Will man prevail? Who can say? We live in Hope.

JAMES C. COURTNEY   15

An older man may look back upon his youthful, romantic adventures and "conquests" with a pleasant nostalgia. But if he should ever try to recapture those feelings he will fail. He will know embarrassment and regret, do irreparable damage to those enjoyable memories and end as a fool.

***

When one is in a bleak mood; when nothing seems worth doing and all avenues seem closed to us we must simply stop. Do nothing. Wait. Given time, duty will begin to appear all about us. The things we must do we will do. We will soon be back into action and, as we know, action drives out depression. Thank God for our bountiful store of obligations.

***

If you marry a second time, choose a mate who is very different from your first. Avoid any thoughts of comparison, be they favorable or no, lest you slide back into the quagmire from which you have so recently struggled to emerge. This is a second chance! Enter the second marriage as a person created anew.

***

Be loyal to your friends. Cultivate them as though they were priceless, ornamental flowers. And as they are loyal, loving company in your lifetime they will be eloquent eulogizers at your funeral.

***

Some say that we should redistribute a portion of our wealth among the poorer of our fellow humans. Some say we must keep the wealth and let the poor help themselves. Yet if we do nothing then the poor will indeed presently help themselves in unexpected ways that may cause our placid world to erupt.

—

"Blood and destruction shall be so in use
And dreadful objects be so familiar
That mothers will but smile when they behold
Their infants quarter'd with the hands of war".
Shakespeare *Julius Caesar*

***

Try to live near flowing water: a river, a stream, a brook or a creek. It will become a clock, reminding you constantly of the passage of time. It is alive and will live on long after you have become a memory. Watch the river. It will whisper, "Bustle! Make hay! Grasp hold of life! Leap into life or leap into me"!

***

Do not wait to be "called". Choose your path and go forth straightway. To select the wrong path will be a mistake that may be mended. To fail to move, fail to venture forth in search of yourself, is to become lost in a backwater swamp; slowly decaying; awaiting your demise: a stranger to yourself.

***

"Constructive criticism" of a friend has cost more friendship than fisticuffs. A man is usually aware of his deficiencies. He would rather not be reminded of them; especially by a close friend. Let his doctor, lawyer or spiritual advisor deal with the defects of your friend. Instead, concentrate upon reminding him of his value to you as a companion and a "brother". You will both be happier.

***

I have noticed that the most persistent medical advice comes to me from men who are alcoholics, drug users, tobacco smokers, incompetent automobile drivers and/or women chasers. Several of these are victims of adult diabetes, have undergone multiple heart attacks, cardiovascular implants, "by-passes", minor amputations and more. Yet they advise me about exercise, vitamins and pills to stimulate my sex drive. And these are my *friends*!

***

Chocolate, in any and all its forms and textures, is the food for me. I decide which will be for tonight: dark, light, Belgian, Swiss, nut bar or cherry filled, wine flavored or caramelized. Then I build my dinner around my selection.

***

Surgeons earn more in one hour than I do in three months. Pay attention to your General Practitioner and trust him but beware of surgery. Your Doctor is your loyal shipmate. The Surgeon is a privateer whose face you never see and who will pass from you to another surgery, forgetting your name before he has washed his hands.

***

Let him who passionately desires a special woman take care. He should first read about the habits of the praying mantis.

**

Civility should be practiced only upon the civilized.

**

Our children are our most precious gifts. We are theirs. The difference is that only we parents are aware of this symbiosis.

**

The most beautiful face you will ever see covers a grisly skull. Cherish the charm while it lasts, love it as it ages and kiss the beloved face that has grown old. Venerate the ones lost to death; even as they decay.

**

A carousel completes one rotation as it slowly spins on the action-filled midway. Each turn presents a different view to the rider. So each day is freshly new and important. That is why the Earth turns; to give us another day, another view, another chance. Welcome to another spin! Good day to you, my friend!

**

The two masks of theater represent comedy and tragedy. Life itself might be depicted in the same way but with a third mask; this of a blank expression, representing most of the time.

**

A man who loves all beautiful women has much to keep him busy. For a new crop ripens every year and there are a finite number of nights.

**

A friend has observed: In golf, when you hit a long shot that comes within inches of the flag stick, your fellow golfers pronounce it "a truly great shot!" But when the same shot results in the ball dropping into the cup, you are branded as "Lucky!" The first draws generous applause; the second, howls of laughter!

**

Life is a tragedy, punctuated now and then by the comedic acts of serious men.

**

First, care assiduously for your health. For if you do not look after yourself you may not be able to take care of the ones you love.

**

The best form of government is one that is always on the edge of revolution. It listens. It acts quickly to fulfill the needs of the people. A regime which ignores the masses (when aroused), will finally step over the edge into oblivion. Given time, the enraged populace will inevitably devour the tyrant.

**

We learn to write by reading. We learn to live by the processes of living.

**

To calm the passion of hate, fear or love there is nothing like a good night's rest. But for remorse there is no termination outside the grave. The cure for such regret, deferred for a time, is found only in the Long Nap.

**

A shrewd leader always placates his military forces. He feeds them and houses them and provides for their general well-being. The supreme monarch needs a loyal army; else his crown sits in constant jeopardy.

**

Avoid emotional arguments at all costs. Rage drives out reason and it is only through reason that we can hope to instruct the ignorant. Be calm and even silent in the face of fury. It is quite possible that an uneducated man may rant long enough to stumble into right thinking without your help.

**

When dining with a beautiful woman she is truly a feast to the eyes. And later, when you are alone with her, as you would approach a sumptuous buffet, you hardly know where to start.

**

When a man has seen even one of his children grow to become a fine adult, he can be justly proud. It is as if he had been honored with a statue in the town square; a grand memorial to his own life.

**

Objects closest to explosions suffer the most damage. Those closest to us suffer the most from our carelessness, indifference and rage. Be careful.

**

Sing a song. Sing off key or off beat or sing with the voice of a bird or an angel or a frog. But sing along with the wind and the rustling leaves, the brook and the waterfall. Sing with the crow and the cricket. Sing along with the thunder. Sing with the whistle of the freight train and the toot of the barge. All is well when you join your voice to the songs of your world.

***

Visit the zoo to learn about man. Watch the mother lion play with her cubs and cuff them gently when they bite. See the panda do a somersault. Wonder as the chimpanzees play and love like us; only with more honesty. See the school of fishes swim in unison without having to rehearse. Watch the tiger dozing by his dinner. See the bear, closed off from his home in the snowy hills far away. See the eagle mewed up. See the cages and the bars and the food trays and the shovels and the gawkers and the popcorn strewn about. See the cameras and balloons. See the children laugh at the tenants, shut up on display. And watch the people. Go to the zoo to learn about the people.

***

Religious arguments persist. Often sectarian wars erupt. Genocide and murder have supplanted reality and logic and thus have kept the grave-diggers busy. The religious faithful continually stumble about, allowing superstition to obscure logic; disputing over which is "The True Faith". They rant; careless of the carnage; oblivious to the certain arrival of the next, killer asteroid.

***

Beware of the flatterer. The more he praises you the more tightly you should grip your purse.

***

When brothers fight, their quarreling reveals every aspect of an entire family history. So civil wars make clear the long smoldering antipathy between one segment of a society and its coequal opposite. In each case the coals of war require a long time to cool; while ever ready to re-ignite when winds blow awry.

***

Evil, Temptation and Sin. These are the elements that keep religions alive. For without them what would preachers have to say? We already know about love, pain, sacrifice, guilt and atonement. Let the preachers instruct each other.

***

DROPS OF WATER, GRAINS OF SAND

In every aspect of her physical beauty I could discover no imperfection. Her voice was the melodic sound of the cello and the flute. She moved across the room like a long legged cheetah stepping through the forest. Eyes like green jewels set in ivory cheekbones and long, black hair cascading to her shoulders; scarlet lips parting into a bejeweled, sparkling smile; her laughter like church bells; in all these she was perfection. Then I married her.

***

It is quiet in winter. We walk less and are more careful of the slippery spots. Cars drive more slowly. Lovers cuddle by the fireplace. Children play indoor games. The windows and doors of my house are closed up mostly and the snow itself muffles the sounds of the winds. It is a time to think; to plan for Spring when the commotion will return. And by Spring we are anxious for the excitement of planning for summer. We are creatures of the weather as surely as are the migratory birds. There are no purposeless seasons.

***

The most convincing liar carries within him the instrument of his self-destruction: a propensity toward self-deception.

***

We will lose friends. A thoughtless word, an omitted compliment, a careless insult; these can cost us the companionship of friends. Death steals friends from us; most often by their deaths and someday, only once, our own. But friends are often lost as a small coin is misplaced; through inattention. A friendship needs nourishment. Tend to your friends lest they find another tender and, seeking them, you discover that they are too busy for you.

***

The emotion of love makes us most vulnerable. For those whom we love exert a power over us that we would not normally, willingly grant to anyone; except, perhaps, to God. Indeed, to love someone perfectly is to make sacrifice to them: to make of them a god. And what are we to them?

***

Everyone should have a favorite, classic novel. Read it first in your twenties and again every decade or so from then on. With each reading the story will seem to have changed a bit. This reflects the changes in your own vision. What it will mean to you each time will be a much modified and a new adventure; thus a reflection of your own, inner evolution.

***

The most hilarious joke told at the wrong time, in the wrong place, to the wrong people can become a painfully embarrassing catastrophe. Pick your spots.

***

Some lessons are learned soon, with one or two teachings: stoves can burn, bees can sting, a dull knife can still cut a finger. Other principles take longer to comprehend: politicians may lie, friends may betray, your dog may bite you and true love may not last forever. Such lessons learned rarely require repeating.

***

Without a dream man is but a beast obediently dragging his burdens.

***

It is November. The leaves are strewn across the fields, the corn stalks stand withering in the wind. Bright, light summer clothing is put away to be replaced by the dark, heavy raiments of winter. The trees seem embarrassed by their nudity. Firewood is stacked by the stove and a cup of coffee does not stay warm for long.

One day, from out of the west, a thick, black blanket of clouds rides in on roaring winds. All night long the gale pounds the cabin; sneaks in through cracks we thought we'd sealed. Finally silence. We sleep. In the early morning we look outside to find our land bedecked with a downy blanket of the whitest snow. Everything out there looks clean. The barn roof, the shattered fence, the broken tractor kept for parts, the fields and the far away hills and even the sky; all these are bright and clear, soft and beautiful. My mother calls me to a hot breakfast. This is a good place to live!

***

I watch the pendulum swing. The old clock was indeed my grandfather's. I learned to wind it and to set the time when I was but a child of ten or so. Sometimes now, I pretend that each click is a minute and thus imagine an hour passes by in short time. Suppose each sequence were an hour or a day! Then how fast time would fly! To God, each oscillation of that swinging brass fixture may be an eon. Is there an end to time? But right now my chores await me.

***

He who laughs last is most likely hard of hearing or dull of wit. Or both.

***

Fences. They break the landscape into grids. They mar the grassland with their posts and wires. They incarcerate the animals and domesticate God's creatures so we may sheer them or freely kill and eat them. The fences segregate men from each other. They are used to punish criminals and protect the populace. There are even fences around playgrounds and church yards. They keep me in and they keep me out. A world of fences and walls. Every fence has its purpose, I suppose. I must learn to accept the ugliness.

***

Pity the man who does not value poetry. He will most likely lack an appreciation for music as well. Music and poetry spring from the same place in the psyche of man. The need to move away from cold reality into an ethereal site impels some people to write music and poetry. We who hear or read the product of their efforts are, for the moment, lifted up with them. Along with music and poetry was born man's first urge to fly.

***

To spend time in a foreign country is to discover within yourself aspects of your nature which had been previously concealed. We travel outward on a quest to discover what is inside us. We almost always succeed.

***

"psychosomatic: **2.** of the mind and body together." I prefer to think of the mind and body in conflict rather than "together", except in the meaning that two boxers in the same ring are "together". The mind and body do, indeed, battle. The body, with a regular and unrelenting drumbeat, instructs us as to what our wants, "needs", desires, comforts and unrecognized instincts *require*. The body says "Require," but the mind is filled with "should" and "ought" and "do not" and "avoid" and "thou shalt" and "thou shalt not". It is no wonder that psychiatrists abound and thrive, endeavoring daily to resolve these conflicts within their patients while, in their spare time, working out these same problems for themselves. They live in big houses, drive fast cars, travel to Hawaii for conventions, write best-selling books and are the most likely group of all medical doctors to commit suicide.

***

Some lessons need to be taught over and over. For the mind may learn what the body will reject or forget. The body has a will of its own and the mind has no body. Confusing? How often must our body be re-taught that a quart of whiskey is too much and that the lust for one woman is enough?

***

Early to bed and early to rise makes Jack a dull boy.

***

My favorite book is the one I am reading now. My favorite song is the one I'm hearing now. My favorite woman is the one waiting for me now. Excuse me.

***

When I am in Church on Sunday I notice the vestments of the priest and who is serving as altar boy, and I note the absence or presence of certain fellow parishioners. I mouth the hymn of the day and determine by my watch how long the sermon has lasted and how soon I may arrive at the lake behind my home. Once there, in my small boat, ceremoniously waving my line out in rhythm, fishing for something or nothing, smelling the water, feeling the breeze and the sun, contemplating the secrets of the pond; it is only then that I begin to think of God. It is only then that I begin to emit prayers of thanks.

***

Among my several recurring nightmares is the one wherein my friend, the lawyer, while visiting my home, slips and falls.

***

Of all the sad things in life, the most lamentable is that we do not learn to appreciate the value of life until we have lost a loved one to death.

***

The pilgrim travels out to the place he has sought all his life. Once there, he absorbs every aspect of the locale. He walks the streets, touches the statues and listens to the sounds. Upon his return he contemplates. Home is still home. His image in the mirror remains unmodified. Yet he has been profoundly and forever altered.

***

Never believe the word, "Unbreakable". It is a lie.

***

We visit cemeteries to bury our friends and to remember our lost loved ones. A cemetery may become a place of sadness. But there is also a celebratory aspect to be found there. We are reminded of the treasure of life which we possess right now. We are living the gift of life. The best way to pay reverence to the dead is to live. We stride from the graveyard with renewed purpose.

***

DROPS OF WATER, GRAINS OF SAND

Let's just start the war! Let the guns roar and the body count commence! Load up the hospitals and glut the graveyards! Come on Stock Market! (Buy wooden limbs, caskets and headstones.) I need the money! I have only two houses and my neighbor has *three*!

***

I stride the narrow, stone streets of an old city, far from home. I do not speak the local language nor do I know a soul in town. But I have more in common with those generations who lived here, past and present, than I do with my neighbor back at home. I am not alone. I am on my way to a one thousand year old place of worship. My shoes tread a familiar, well worn path.

***

My grandfather was a coal miner who, after years of scratching and blasting and loading coal, rose to the level of shift boss and never went back down inside. He kept his son out of those mines with stern admonitions and a brutal slap on the backside if he even spoke of a thought of shaft mining. (Almost all Dad's pals became miners.) Grandpa's son went to school. My father became a fine lawyer. Both those men are dead now and I am old. I live in a fine home by a quiet stream. My son is a successful businessman with a lovely wife and three fine daughters. Thank you, grandpa. I'm sorry I never met you.

***

Never plan too far ahead. The events of a day or an hour may cause your objectives to change. The Future itself is the only sure objective. It will arrive. Work toward the future. Perform every duty with dedication. Pay close attention to your loved ones. Your hopes and dreams (along with pain and hardship), will appear on schedule and they will almost always be a surprise.

***

To be successful in the stock market one must be immersed in the study of the herd mentality in all its complexities. Infiltrate the herd. Associate with the herd, adopt the dress, language and deportment required. But, at all costs, avoid becoming a *bona fide* member of the herd.

***

Lust for Power, Acquisition of Power, Repression, Social Unrest, Anarchy, Revolution, Reconstruction, New Order, New Laws, New Leaders, New Lusts. Round and round they go pell-mell and where they stop no one can tell.

***

When is a lady not a lady? When she is alone with the man she loves.

**

If you can explain in detail why you love someone (give a list of reasons), then you are probably not in love. For true love has nothing to do with facts but with feelings, and feelings have always defied and eluded verbal expression.

**

No one ever got paid for being smart. No one was ever knighted for being intelligent. It is finally deeds that reward us, not thoughts. Genius is sometimes a necessary but never a sufficient component of greatness. The framers of The United States Constitution were wise men but are well remembered for what they did and not for what they thought. It is not enough to think. We must perform deeds which then may impel others (and ourselves) to further action. For it is actions that change the world; sometimes for the better.

**

Think first. Only then act; or don't act. Any other sequence is folly and has caused more regret than all the wars in history, many of which might have been avoided if men had followed the axiom: "Think first".

**

All forms of art that we know are representational (or strive to become non-representational to little effect). Only music is the thing itself. Only in music can we hope to express and understand Art. Music can cross cultures and, if failing completely to accomplish that, can be understood for what it means to the culture from which it comes. A piece of music defies discussion. There it is, on lined paper, waiting to be experienced anew. "All art strives to become music." *(anon)*

**

A luckless duck has allowed himself to be trapped; frozen in an ice layer suddenly formed on the river last night. He cries out for help. I cannot walk out on the thin, snow covered layer to help him. Yet I care. His quacking siblings on the bank care. Who can save him? He calls to the Sun God for warmth to melt his prison. He looks to me for help. We all pray together. His struggles and God's mercy prevail. There is joy about the pond. My little pal is free.

**

A preemptive war is like a preemptive execution. It is the product of arrogance. "I think this man may kill. Therefore execute him immediately"!

***

We are often admonished to, "Live in the moment!" With respect, I suggest that there is no other way to live. We cannot relive the past or predict or shape the future. We plan and dream and work for tomorrow and then tomorrow just happens; paying almost no attention to our expectations. Tomorrow is a mystery and yesterday is a memory. It is today that counts. Be grateful for today and, with enthusiasm, use it up.

***

When I feed the birds and the various critters that inhabit my yard, am I upsetting Nature's selection process? I like to think I am helpful and that these dumb creatures appreciate my aid this winter. Perhaps they think I am God? A noble, if lofty, aspiration for an otherwise ineffectual man.

***

Today I received a *Thank You* note from a friend. I performed a small favor for him and he thanked me. We are more than even. We are friends.

***

When I was young I dreamed of many things; I had many wants which, over time, seemed as needs. I struggled on: acquiring: Now, finally, I have every thing I dreamed of... except my wasted and forever lost youth.

***

In front of my house, down by the creek, a tree tilts toward the water. Its roots are dead. It is likely to tumble in at the next rain. I will have to cut it down soon before it falls. I regret the labor that lies ahead for me, but this is a must. I think about sharpening my ax. I doze after dinner. Then to bed. And yes! This morning I see that the old tree has indeed fallen over and is gone; washed away forever! You see, if you wait long enough, your problems will solve themselves. Do not rush to your chores. Give Time and Nature a chance. All good things come to the slothful!

***

The exciting discovery you can make is not gold or diamonds or a kingdom of your own. The prize is hidden inside your brain. It is an idea that enthuses you, fills you with a drive for accomplishment, motivates you with seemingly boundless energy. Yet it will not be the achievement of that objective that is your prize but the invigorating thrill of the urgent pursuit.

***

We watch our grandchildren take their first steps. We hear them laugh. We listen with rapt attention as they speak to us in unintelligible gibberish and smile at them with approval and a feigned understanding as they point up to a bird or a puff of cloud. We recognize ourselves. They are simply us as we were. We inhale aspects of our own immortality.

**

The principles of accounting stress the "bottom line": the "profit" or the "loss". These terms have crept into our vernacular and are now used to describe social situations, logical quandaries and human relationships in general. This is an error of the first order. Humans defy equations. To speak of a "bottom line" with respect to humans is to reduce them to pure numbers; statistical units which can be manipulated into an equation and thus dropped into slots befitting their "value". Sociologists too have a tendency to turn man into groupings of factoids. Such generalizations will not illuminate the nature of man. Man is more complex than any science known to man.

**

Little boys play with toy guns, cars, trucks, trains, planes, etc. Little girls play with dolls, dollhouses, toy cookery, lipstick and their mother's shoes. Each is practicing to become an adult. Watch them grow and you will see. Woe to the parent (and his child), who tries to change that pattern.

**

I never saw a skinny sloth. Did you? They must be doing something right.

**

The older I get the more I hear voices advising me to live life to the fullest. Those voices seem to come from the graves of my departed loved ones.

**

On the scale of one's lifetime, *style* has a very a short duration. A *fad* lasts about one tenth as long as a style. Create your own style and alter it only as and when you would alter yourself.

**

Being right in matters of morality is important. Being seen to be right is much less important. For what joy is to be found when fools praise your judgment and scoundrels count you as a friend? That is unless you are a politician; in which case perception is everything and morals be hanged.

**

News reporters boast that they supply the "who, what, when, where" and even "how". But after the stories have been shoved off the front page, to be replaced by more sensational news, we, the thinking readers, are always left with the unaddressed question: "Why?" Why that suicide? Why the arsonist or bomber did what he did. Why this war at this time? Why some actor in California uses cocaine! Why the rape in our town? Why the serial killer? And no one knows why, or even if we readers care.

***

The impulse to reproduce is of prime importance to all animate things; from the alga to the orchid, from earthworms to humans. Important as this is to the continuation of a species, why must laws be enacted which codify so many social and religious restrictions upon the reproductive activities of its human members? We too are impelled by that drive! We simply must survive! To believe in God is to revere His plan and to allow for His wide diversity. He loves us even as we explore.

***

Mothers play a disproportionate role in the development of their sons until about the age of twelve or so. Then the father's role becomes more influential and it grows. It is hoped that the lessons learned from the father are not too different from those taught by the mother. A drastic reversal of teachings can lead to confusion, anguish, anxiety and mental problems of varying degrees. Let the father and mother consult and work together to achieve an orderly transfer of power. It is their son whose future is at stake.

***

I loved Lilly. I held back on a commitment to marry her until I had concluded my education. The wait was too long for her. She was ripe and much sought after. I lost her to another, less cautious man. My education continued. I received a law degree and met and married Alice. I still think of Lilly. The practice of law can be unfulfilling. It is too late. I wonder if I did the right thing. I wonder where Lilly is tonight and if she ever thinks of me.

***

A man who cannot endure loneliness is not to be trusted in society.

***

Memory is an excellent instructor but a harsh jurist. Through experience it can teach us moral rectitude while constantly harassing us with indictments for our past sins. Memory is the sword of two edges.

***

The monies I had saved for an exciting retirement lie in the bank. The places to which I would have traveled are now too crowded. The cost of everything is now too high. I am more tired than I had thought I would be. The news in the papers frightens me. I must now save my money for the doctor bills sure to come. My heirs frequently check on my health. What happened?

***

Here's to all the composers and musicians! They make the music that excites, relaxes, soothes, inspires us; calls up the hero within us, aids us in expressing bereavement as well as in our joyful moments. Music: the voice of the soul. Music: without which the world would be only barely bearable. Play on!

***

Tally all the wars ever fought between nations. Add up all the dead and wounded, the widows and orphans and reflect upon the usual pointlessness of these battles. It is sad. Yet sadder still is Man's relentless battle against Nature. Man has never won nor never will he win a struggle against Nature. Man is but a minuscule component of Nature and, as such, has yet to master even himself. In such a struggle man's only "winning" will be the destruction of Nature entirely. Who will there be to declare Victory?

***

When I looked into her wide eyes I saw myself as I had always wished to be. I saw what I might become and I was pleased. I was then compelled to make of myself the man she had envisioned and thus to make her mine.

***

As in science and religion so in politics and war; the focus is on the differences between contending parties. If somehow, someday, the attention could be diverted to the sameness of the competitors (the scores of areas of general agreement), and away from their often petty disputes, the energy thus redirected could be used to solve a world of problems. We are indeed like little brothers, often squabbling over shiny, worthless trinkets.

***

DROPS OF WATER, GRAINS OF SAND

The riddle of man and woman has no solution. They are drawn together and yet must remain apart. A man's view of the world is macro while woman's is micro. Man provides; Woman cares, Man plants the seeds, Woman nurtures the crops. Man wars while Woman nurses the wounded and mourns the dead. The separate roles of the sexes seem obvious and the lines appear sharply drawn. Yet this is not so. For in every man there is to be found a female component and what woman is not capable of performing man's duties as and if required? Situations prevail. The only way to establish the only definitive difference between the sexes is to study a book on anatomy. From that inquiry may be drawn inferences but not conclusions.

***

The death of a child is an insult to our view of the order of things. It saddens us; maddens us to see our offspring lying in that grave where, by rights, we should be. At this time we are either consoled by our Faith or we excise religion from our lives altogether; counting random chance as the only certainty.

***

Life is the winning of a million to one chance in a lottery. Life itself is both a jackpot and a trophy. We rejoice at the miracle and defend with vigor the honored prize. And Death? It is certain; and only a minor price to pay for the privilege of living.

***

Old folks learn to live alone. No matter their circumstances, as they age they retreat into themselves. The memories from this morning fade away as thoughts of long ago emerge, to march along with old sounds and colors, laughter and tears, pride, regret and wonder. They still can wonder.

***

A river knows what to do with a rain storm that lasts for days. It speeds up, widens, gashes a new course, perhaps, then floods the dry land. Then it recedes and becomes its familiar self. The folks along the river understand this oscillating process. They watch the rain and the river and they move to higher ground; watch more and wait. Then they return to clean up such mess they find. But will they move away? Never. They understand the river. The flood brings fresh earth for spring planting and all the wells are full again. It will be a good year. So it is that people live with Nature. Pity him who demands of Nature that She conform to *his* wishes and woe to the man who ravages his Mother.

***

When Judgment Day comes I will not ask for justice. (One cannot fool the Judge!) I plan to beg for mercy. I am even now composing my plea.

***

One of the many reasons that grandchildren are so beloved by their parent's parents is that we can lavish the little ones with praise and love and leave the table manners, grooming lessons and discipline to our grown children.

***

Motion pictures have been one of my most efficient instructors. Tales of heroes and villains, voyages of discovery, legendary love stories, values lost or found, betrayal, redemption, wars and peace. This is what we are taught in school, (and in life), but the movie theater is more conducive to retained lessons than a classroom and much less painful than learning through life.

***

There is a mysterious anomaly in the mouth. Why do we have thirty-two teeth when the mouth can hold only twenty-eight? And why do they call those extra four teeth "Wisdom Teeth"? The only "wise" lesson to be found is to have them removed before they abscess and poison us. (Did God do this to us in order to provide a secure stream of income to dentists?)

***

It makes sense that a doctor might be an atheist. He is surrounded by pain and death and weeping and despair, only partially offset by the his regular, expected successes. Hence a healer might become a cynic or even think himself a god if he is treated as such and only rarely fails. I suspect that every young surgeon feels godlike and every mature doctor prays to God every day.

***

As a patient, seek a young diagnostician and a mature surgeon. With the two you have contemporary science mated with skilled and seasoned experience. This is also true of automobile mechanics.

***

When a woman falls in love with another woman it is sometimes termed by men a disgrace or even a perversion. But in truth all men are merely sad. For two women have thus been removed from the quarry pool.

***

If ever trapped in small quarters for a long time with a talkative person, let him speak on. Feed him the fodder of even more subjects for his babbling. He will talk forever anyway, therefore you have a right to select the subjects. That way you can, perhaps, learn a thing or two woth knowing about a subject which interests you.

**

When I am dead, place my body in an aged, leaking canoe. Set it loose upon a wide and rushing river. We are both now fit for the trash heap but we ask for honor while passing there. Send us drifting down the river so that we may reach the sea. Let the tides bear us out and the waves wash us down. Let us sink into the silence of our ancestral, salty home. We will surely be welcome there.

**

I am too old to be the captive of my passions. Yet I am not so old as to forget them. What joy and excitement in fulfillment and what sadness in the disappointments that followed. The emotional peaks and valleys were wondrous, but like strenuous, contact sports, designed for the young. I am alone now with my hammock and my memories. There is no one at home to greet me and no one left to mourn. I am in a "holding pattern".

**

I do not curse in front of women; it is coarse and impolite. Yet I often curse, blaspheme and swear. I may even resort to street language on occasion. Any man who tries to prevent me form "blowing off steam" by my choice of words, (when he can plainly see that my vexation has become dangerously powerful), is no man at all. He is a woman.

**

More outrages are practiced by leaders of organized religion than are found among the heathens of the world. (Still the faithless cast about for faith.) God will not long suffer this insult. Hell was designed with hypocrites in mind.

**

I sometimes feel lonely for no good reason. I am reminded then of the person who wrote: "There is no loneliness so bleak as that which one feels when lying in bed next to someone whom one no longer loves. (*anon.*)" I sleep alone.

**

Romantic love is Nature's way of saying, "Make a baby and get on with it!" To interpret things any other way is to delude one's self. But what is love anyway but joyous, luxuriant, unforgettable, fulfilling, inescapable self-delusion?

***

Predictability is possible only by examination of the past and close scrutiny of the present. Even then, one must be prepared for surprises.

***

When one writes, he chooses his words with care, checks his grammar and spelling, phrases his objective with precision, prints it out and dispatches it at once. It is carefully read and understood for what it says. But no one knows what the careful writer truly thinks.

***

I built a fire in the fireplace last night. Outside it was so cold that the icicles trembled. Soon the cabin was warm and I removed my sweater. Then the place grew warmer so I opened the door; just a crack. Then I poured a glass of water and doused a bit upon my face. Why the fire, so sweet-scented, crackling and warm? Because I like a warm fire on a cold night.

***

It seems to me that men in power want the rest of us to act "sensibly". To act "sensibly" is to do what is expected of us by others. What is sensible to one man may be folly to another. Let each man think as he pleases, whether it "makes sense" or not. The powerful take care of themselves and each other. Let the rest of us take care of ourselves as we see fit. Men of great power often act out of caprice. Are we not allowed our whims?

***

To fly over The Rain Forest is sublime. To travel the rivers of The Rain Forest is exhilarating. To camp all night on the banks of those rivers is terrifying. To study the flora and fauna of The Rain Forest is to see the hand of God. Then to live for a time among the few indigenous tribes remaining in The Rain Forest is to regain admiration for all mankind. Let them have their trees!

***

Give me the author who writes as he speaks. Soon I shall know the man and feel comfortable with his views. I may not agree but I will know he is espousing his honest perspective of reality and I will esteem him. I will trust him.

***

Every morning one should smile at a stranger. The very act makes him feel better and always lightens one's own step. Someone may even smile back. Or that person may carry the smile on to another. Your smile may be passed on, like a baton, from one runner to the next; making the day a rousing sporting race for many rather than a dismal toil of one.

***

All death should be sudden. It should strike when we are in the peak of health, having experienced, as yet, no disintegration of our bodies. Death should come to us in the hour of our successful completion of a great task or a bountiful journey; when we feel most powerful. We should be among friends. Death should come at a moment of intense and excited anticipation. We should be thinking about the glory to come and of the embrace of our waiting loved ones who will soon be at our side. Death should be stealthy as an assassin, lurking in the shadows outside our view, and he should kill swiftly; with the accuracy of a seasoned marksman.

***

Survivors talk of wars. Generals write of wars. The rotting casualties (soldiers and civilians) have a somewhat different view of battle. Ah, but they lie mute.

***

Certain fantastic, horror tales are told and retold to each generation. They often are presented in a night-shrouded atmosphere. We are to believe that strange things happen in the night while we innocents sleep. Yet there is nothing supernatural about the night and the many activities peculiar to the night. Night is quiet and thus provides for peaceful rest for humans, most animals and green plants. However it is a fact that certain animals hunt in the night: raccoons, gerbils, bush babies, bats, margays, ocelots, opossums, gila monsters, Tasmanian devils and Dracula.

***

The Wealthy buy the Politicians who control the army and give tax credits to The Church, so that The Church may pacify the poor by teaching them about a better afterlife. The Church instructs its members to tolerate the following: their own, mean condition, The Wealthy, The Politicians and a multitude of injustices. So sectarian societies become the Dictatorships of the Wealthy, the Security of The Politicians and the Protection of the Church. I assume God is displeased with this situation. I know I am.

***

Disobedient Pandora! She released all the evils of the world from the forbidden jar and thousands of years later they still roam about, causing everything from wars to plagues to boils. But she replaced the lid just before Hope was released. Hope remains. We can all still hope. Every day we should give thanks to that inquisitive lady, as day after day we are ever in need of Hope.

***

In some societies men and women wear their age with pride; as a badge of honor. This is honest and good. We in the West have an unhealthy craving for perpetual youth! Why the hair dye and the make-up kit? Are we play-actors? Hang the plastic surgeons and flog the cosmetologists from the city!

***

Just as every event is both the result of a cause and a precursor to the future, so there are no uncaused events and no event which is not also a cause. Similarly, every story told has an antecedent and does indeed have a following narrative. Life will always be a mystery to those who do not look backward for causes and forward with a view toward effects. Indeed, answers can be found, if ever, only in the past and accurate predictions of the future are dependent upon both the past and the present. A story removed from the context of its history is incomplete and is of no use now or in the future.

***

Young lovers see each other as realized dreams and perfection come to life. It is from such fantasies that the great romantic plays are derived and from which the next generation strolls onto the stage. Who would disabuse these lovers of their illusions? Who would sacrifice his own birth in order to repeal the requisite laws of romance? Such a man would, of course, be absent.

***

Any lesson worth learning is worth learning over and over until you get it right.

***

Listen closely to the ravings of the lunatic. He is trying to tell you something but in a manner unintelligible to you. Should you learn to decode his gibberish you might discover the secrets of the universe or how to turn a solid sphere inside out. Listen closely to him but do not follow his advice on any matter.

***

It is typical of a man running for political office that he will greet you with a wide smile and, as he shakes your hand, quickly shift his eyes away toward his next target. This is the way of both the active candidate and the seasoned sniper.

***

At three score and ten I still practice the lessons taught me by my mother when I was five or so: "Go to the bathroom now whether you have to or not. Wash your hands whether you want to or not. Use your napkin at all meals. At least, taste everything. Do not smack your lips. Smile when we adults smile. Say 'please' and 'thank you' and when guests leave be sure to say, 'come back'.

***

A politician correctly feels that: "Even Jesus Christ cannot change things unless he gets elected." Of course this truism is then perverted and is quickly translated, through the ego, to mean: "I have the answers to the problems. Therefore I am within my rights, nay, it is my *duty*, regardless of the law, to do whatever it takes to get elected." Getting elected is the first and only respected law of the candidate: the second and only law is to get re-elected.

***

Old men speak of "the good, old days" with such affection, forgetting the many problems encountered then and absent now. Even younger men sometimes yearn for their school days, forgetting how they hated this class or that teacher. It is the young and the very young who look forward. Old man, follow the young into tomorrow. You will both need each other. Hold hands tightly.

***

War begins before the first shot is fired and does not end until all dead are buried. That is a long duration for a war. Almost every generation has its wars. It seems hard to squeeze a bit of peace in between the wars.

***

Nepotism is the enemy of capitalism because it robs the system of its first law: open competition. Furthermore, it is the enemy of any enterprise to the extent that pure merit is ignored. It stunts the recipient because it robs him of his own, personal quest; to follow his own, untrod path toward his own goal; to slay his own dragons. Finally, it is the enemy of the well-intentioned benefactor because it robs him of an independent, self sufficient, bold and confident son.

***

Let life have meaning first to us. Forget about wills, endowments, the church, the headstone and the graveyard. Forget the eulogies. Simply live in such a way as to be faithful to yourself and your dreams. Live so as to face death as a new, exciting chapter in your life, or perhaps, as nothing; the void. Life is about living as a book is about reading and a song is about singing. Life has the meaning we give to it now. It's your life. Define it for yourself; then live it.

***

While falling in love is not as requisite to procreation as are the organs of the body, it is the best precursor of successful child rearing. Enduring, romantic love can make the process of living and dying more bearable.

***

Do not go south for the winter. The sun goes south and most birds go south, but most mammals stay home, prepared for the splendid harshness of winter. Better to confront the season. Nap by the fireplace supplied by the wood you cut last summer and cuddle with a loved one and sip hot chocolate. Grow a beard. Grow a thin layer of fat. Crunch through the icy yard to feed the squirrels. Man does not need to migrate; he holds his ground. And when spring comes, as it always does, experience the joy and the pride of having come through it all, once more victorious. Say what you will about winter but you must admit it is a ruggedly handsome, worthy, sparring partner.

***

There are men who are lonely in a crowded room and happily gregarious when alone in their study with pen and paper. These men may write odes to love or sonnets to a phantom lady or they may praise marriage with their pen. These men make very poor husbands. They are totally self-absorbed egoists.

***

The bells are ringing. The Christmas tree is lighted. The presents lie ready to be opened and songs are sung. No photo can capture the essence of the moment and few memories will be retained for long. But we must try. These happy times fly away while the Earth orbits but a few times. Remember the togetherness, for too soon we will all depart.

***

There are some invitations extended in such a manner as to be correctly regarded as rejections.

***

War drums beat. Blood runs faster through our veins. The enemy rides toward us from that far-off hill. Many will die, they and we together. We sharpen our spears and call upon God for his aid. Both sides pray to the same God for victory. Remind me. What is this war about? Is this a new war or an old one resurrected? But hurry! Here they come!

***

I wasted my university years. I loafed and drank and chased the girls down the beach. I kept all my books, though, and aging toward dotage, I now read them nightly. I have many questions but no one to answer. I write verses and essays but have no one to critique me: to validate me. I want those years back. Now I realize that they were not about me but about my teachers.

***

I bought a luxurious, foreign sports car. It was a high powered and high-strung vehicle. Maintaining it was costly so I learned to be my own mechanic. I spent a week tuning it but could drive it for only a day or so till it needed more attention. I sold the car and got married. I miss my car. It could be fixed.

***

Society admires and rewards productivity. Much of the populace seeks to find happiness by producing and reaping those rewards and therefore sells itself into bondage. Yet Man is content only when he is free to discover who he is and thereby cut a path through the blizzard of life, pointing outward toward himself. Toil that pays only money is a theft of the soul. Employment that fulfills the spirit is God's preview of Heaven.

***

Despite the cynics and the dreamers, war is not always senseless or an unnecessary evil. It may work, along with Nature, to remove the unfit. The question remains, however, as to who is unfit. Is it the warriors or their leaders? Is it the temporary victors or the apparent vanquished? So wars remain.

***

We raise our glasses to toast the New Year. Are we filled with hope for the year to come or simply glad to see the old year receding? Probably both.

***

It is not enough to be a handsome and convivial suitor. To whom you wish to be the mother of your children, you must present yourself as a model for the man she would choose to be the father of hers.

***

The second son of a landowner, a professional or a peer is merely provisional. He waits in the wings in case he is needed. He is unsure of his purpose in life. He, of all men, is most likely to poison his elder brother.

***

Is it good to have a child? Is it better to have sons or daughters; or both. Better to have one or two children? Five? Ten? I retire to hear the arguments.

***

The Madonna. How many hundreds of different paintings of this mother and child have been produced over the centuries. Surpassing strict religious lines, these images survive in the originals and in millions of reproductions. I believe it is because the image of mother and infant is universal and no child of woman can let his eye wander by without pausing to rest and striving to remember.

***

When I was a young man I used to spend hours preparing for a date with a girl. I often brought flowers to her door. This was the hunt and she was the quarry. The availability of an item has an inverse relationship to its value. Therefore the sexual promiscuity predominant today makes the activity hardly worth bathing, shaving or the price of the popcorn.

***

The theory of evolution, when studied by the philosopher, seems obviously efficient. Things get better over time. The weak leave the stage to the "fittest". Man, seeming to us to be the most adaptable, will therefore survive all other species. It follows that someday we will be alone on Earth. Logic dictates that the "fittest" men will supplant the "weaker" to control the world. What kind of world? What kind of men? Some scientists believe that blue-green algae and the cockroach will be the last to survive. My money is on the flea.

***

I find it difficult to distinguish between a lunatic and a moron and between a maniac and a genius. So do most psychiatrists.

***

Both politicians and logic tell us that war is a last resort. Yet a surprise attack or a preemptive strike or a terrorist offensive reminds us that politicians are not always logical and the prime cause of a war is often obscure, even in history books. To someone, war, in one or more of its guises, was a first option.

**

Always challenge those who seek to dominate your life: especially the Clergy and the Government. They have neither the wisdom nor the right.

**

Mornings are filled with promise. Birds emit arias. The cat and the dog place signs 'round their dominions. We prepare for work or a journey. Mornings are for hope. By noon realism intrudes (as is its duty) and life can get hectic. We survive for the journey back to home. We rest with our loved ones or perhaps alone. We perform a few chores and allow ourselves a portion of relaxation and recreation. We go to sleep. We dream. All in all, not a bad way to exist.

**

> If you're seeking a place that is free from all care,
> Such a place does exist and is easily found.
> There's a man with a hearse who will carry you there;
> To a cold, dark place deep under the ground.

**

Men who see morality in terms of black and white lack both empathy and imagination. They are shackled inside themselves. There are a thousand shades of gray and a rainbow of colors seen every day by the man who knows, loves and lives life; by the man who leaps into life.

**

To bear up under insult requires patience and stoicism. To ignore insult requires wisdom. Only fools respond in kind to fools.

**

A minstrel strolled by yesterday and I stopped my work and sat and listened. He played the lute and sang five songs. I gave him pie and a flask of ale. I pressed a coin into his palm. He left a peacock feather for my hat. So pleasant was the encounter that I judged I'd rather be a meandering minstrel than a member of Parliament. I hope he'll return someday.

**

My beard is white and my gait is slow. I am forgetful, as they told me I might be. But I remember when I was seventeen and took Molly to the dance. I need no photo to picture her. She is as fresh to me today as my gifted orchid was that night. I can almost smell her. I can almost touch her. She has been sixteen for over fifty years. And I am very happy to have held her in my arms that night. Age is not my enemy so much as it is my companion; my history.

***

First teach the child the joy of achieving the possible. Then, in time, now confident, on his own, he will become discontented and attempt the impossible. He just might succeed. This is how innovations and inventions are achieved.

***

Wise men know that "Silence is golden." This is apt because both silence in men and gold in the earth are of about the same rarity.

***

Never rush an education onto others. Some learn more slowly than you, but learning well is more valuable than learning quickly. A parrot can learn The Lord's Prayer in a week but believes that his keeper is God and accounts his daily portion of seeds as manna from the sky.

***

Beyond subsistence, there is little that money can do for one other than provide levels of luxury. To seek the mansion, the yacht, the perceived power of money beyond one's sustenance, yokes one to a life of servitude. His master is money and his burden is having no more important goal in sight as he plods along, pursuing his ever receding objective.

***

He who trusts no one must depend totally upon himself. Yet, as we know, each of us can himself be forgetful, unreliable and self deceptive. Learn to allot certain important matters to others. In our declining years we must learn to trust many others; eventually the gravedigger , the stone cutter and the lawyer.

***

How often does a man wish to have a talk with his father now, these many years after the old man died? They both left so much unsaid.

***

The snows will pile high tonight. The reports tell of a blizzard that will smother all for a day or two. I will be trapped for a time in my home. I have food, water, wood for the fireplace and warm clothes. I have old photo albums and my guitar. I look forward to this wild adventure.

***

All biographies must be placed in an historical context. All history is the sum of many biographies. The story of Man is contained in the biographies of men.

***

There are subjects worth studying which have little to do with science: History, Languages, Literature, Music, Art, and more. There are very few subjects which have nothing to do with science.

***

Dogmatic religions finally must adapt their "truths" to adjust to the facts which science uncovers. Once there was a god of thunder, a god of war and a god for all seasons, etc. Once Earth was believed to be the center of the universe and the Sun but a hot ball, circling Earth; the Sun rose and set upon a flat Earth. Science is for the mind. Religion is of the soul. When the two clash, Religion loses.

***

In reasoning, the narrower the mind the more certain seem the conclusion. Those who believe that their notion of a thing is the only Truth can be found most uniformly in organized religion. A scientist's job is relentlessly to test the ideas of himself and his predecessors with experiments and notions not yet fully examined. The believers move about; arrogantly self-assured and satisfied. The seekers, animated by their imperfect knowledge, searching for absolutes, toil away in their laboratories. Accumulated facts are their bible and Truth is their god.

***

Life Insurance premiums are high and getting higher. It is a bad bet for us because they know the real odds of most events and they set the rates. Their profitability is at stake so the odds are on their side. A casino operates the same way. The difference is that life teaches us to stay out of casinos and to insure ourselves and our property against the unexpected.

***

Each time Religion and Science clash it is science who prevails. Yet science tells us nothing of music, art, literature, history, romantic or paternal love, patriotism or the willingness to die for another; or of the thirst for religion itself. Understanding man is impossible without understanding religion. Religion and Science rule their own separate domains. Let them not constrain each other nor contest by arms lest they both suffer the irreparable loss of the faith of Man.

***

A man who diligently contrives to be well liked by many, may, after time, succeed but he will be inauthentic. He will have forgotten the genuine boy and man he once was. The mask he now wears will be false, ill fitting and permanent. Better to be authentic and to die alone.

***

Marriages arranged by two sets of parents are the most likely, over time, to crumble from within. The young cannot remain faithful to vows uttered by them but imposed by others. Let romantic love rule the union of the young.

***

A mother does not make a credible character witness for her son. In her eyes he is incapable of the crime for which he has been brought before the bar of justice. When she says that he was always a good boy she is not lying. It is just that her recollections are clouded by the habits of loving, forgiving and forgetting .

***

When a man has lost his lover to another through carelessness he is experiencing justice in its most brutal form. It is both immediate and equitable. He will be sentenced to a time in the dungeon of his regret. But there is perhaps another woman out there with the key to his cell. She will release him and he will be more careful with her. This he promises himself.

***

When I was younger I had hope. The hope of the young is boundless and often unrealistic. A much older man now, I have gradually come to terms with reality. There are limits to my abilities and I have lost hope for anything past tomorrow. I miss the foolishness of being eighteen years old.

***

Each religious sect claims to be on the *only* correct path to God. Not only is this fractious and a persistent irritant in the lives of humans, but it must be an embarrassment to The Creator.

***

Excessive food, drink, tobacco and indolence; carelessness with money in the hot pursuit of women; these can significantly shorten one's life. But so can abstinence, diet and worry. So can a religious pilgrimage. The constant attention to one's health and "eternal life" can become a mortal illness.

***

How can one profess a love for and a belief in God and His wisdom and then go out and buy a gun for protection from an imaginary home invader?

***

Jesus taught love, forgiveness, redemption on this Earth as well as in Heaven. He taught the value of peace and joy and of tolerance. It is a tragedy and a shame that today so few "Christians" seem to have learned anything at all from Christ. Christians read His words of love and, like every other religious group, they go forth to let loose carnage upon the world.

***

Those who marry out of passion and romantic love make their vows to each other, their future children and thus to tomorrow. The couple which unites under the guidance and at the behest of their parents pledges loyalty to the parents, to money and to yesterday; as though they were still little children.

***

How boring life would be if we knew the outcome. Perhaps the toil and tedium are for naught, our prayers may speak to a deaf God and our descendants might toss aside our precious legacies. We do not know. What then? We choose to honor our friends and loved ones, but life must be lived for ourselves, knowing full well that, over time, all will be forgotten.

***

How old are those oak trees in the ravine? Are they older than my father born a hundred years ago? His father? Perhaps a Native American couple rested beneath that tree there, planning their future. How many generations of squirrels have been sheltered by that tall, tilting tree by the creek? I stretch a hammock between those twins from which location I can see the blue and white sky and the curious critters staring down at me who think I am trespassing. How many birds call this home? How long will the trees stand after I am dead? These trees should remain; a tribute to the value of all life. I own the land and yet I am but a visitor passing by. The trees have their roots here.

***

To be worth our time, any game of "solitaire" must be easy to learn but difficult to conquer. In life the rules and the direction are laid out for us and are easy to understand, but attaining our goal, (never adequately defined), is never easy. Like the stupefying, random complexities of the deck of cards, life remains a mystery. So we live on; enjoying the solitary game of life.

***

My house is on land high above a small river. Some ducks live here and others use the water for fishing and resting as they conduct their airborne treks north and south with the seasons. It is now the dead of Winter. Yesterday I discovered a female mallard duck on my front deck; no more than two feet on the other side of the glass window; almost one hundred feet above the surface of the river. What was she doing on my deck? I wish she would come back and tell me.

***

Many a picnic is cursed by flies and ants. Winds and blowing sand or dust can cause discomfort. Yet who will ever forget the excitement and the joys of those times when those warm, family gatherings are recalled?

***

Several sources have stated flatly that the Basque language is simply incomprehensible. Two of these linguists have voiced their astonishing theory that due to the complexity of the language, it is probable that no one Basque understands another. Surely this is a jest.

***

I do not pray. God has enough to do without my bothering him. But if I prayed only one prayer it would be something like this: "Dear God, If I could please live this life over I truly believe I would do a better job. Thanks for listening."

***

Some believe that Man arrived on Earth from somewhere out in space. I do not know. But it seems to me that no native of this planet would defile his natural nest as Man does and no Son would treat his Mother with such disrespect.

***

Every plant and animal on Earth has, in the eyes of man, a special purpose in the balance of Nature. Only man himself has been unable to justify his own existence. Inter-species Warrior, Idolater, Master of fire, Killer of whales, and Voyager to the moon. Proud and careless, he creates the Big Boom and then humbly prays to his Idol to be spared from its wrath.

***

Pay heed to the lone protester on the street corner. The man may be a lunatic or a prophet, a fool or a genius. He cries out for peace when you want war. He speaks for the poor and suffers the cat calls of the indifferent. He spends himself, his voice lost upon the wind. But listen. He is trying. You may not agree but you must listen. Good men have died so that he could speak freely.

***

First I noticed. Then I was curious. Then I was attracted. On inspecting more closely I became acquisitive. Then determined; finally grasping and unyielding. Thus I possessed and became possessive. Then began the process of boredom and indifference resulting in carelessness. The object of my former quest was gained, then lost to me (through sale, or gift or by simple misplacement; I forget) and I set about to capture some other prize.

***

Men and women are so different. What draws them together besides the natural need to reproduce the race? A strange symbiosis. A reciprocity. As a pendulum swings from left to right to tell the time, a child looks to mother and to father for the keys to living. A man and woman look to each other for guidance and appreciation. She listens to his dreams and he to her needs. She has her daily chores and he has his. Together in the evening they attend their children's tales and sing the quiet songs and after the children sleep they whisper secrets to each other. They simply love and need one another.

***

For a convicted serial killer in The United States there is often punishment by death. Say he has killed six; yet he dies only once. That's not fair. Since we cannot execute him more than once I suggest we keep him alive and provide such confinement as will protect society from him. See if we might learn from him the secrets of his rage and use the information to partially preclude such violence in the future. No. Society demands vengeance. And vengeance it will have in lieu of knowledge.

***

I have noticed that the victim's family almost always demands strong penalties as a means of providing them with "closure". But when they have sat behind the glass and watched as the execution was carried out, and they are then asked by a newsman if "closure" has been achieved, they usually reply, "No. I suppose there will never be closure." And the hearse is driven away into the darkness to the jeers of the crowd outside the gates.

***

I think Man feels that he does not belong to the Earth. He looks to God for answers to his existence and assurance that there is a place for him somewhere else after he dies. Man ascribes no heaven or hell to any other animal. Despite all the evidence, man thinks of himself as different from and better than all other beasts. Man is, indeed, not comfortable here on Earth. Why did God give us this brain? To make us unhappy? To feel that we do not belong here? All other animals seem to belong. What about us?

***

If God did not want men to catch women then why did he cause women to run so slowly? Their legs are much longer than a greyhound and what man can catch a greyhound? Perhaps women merely lope; wanting to be captured by the certain man they want to capture. God usually knows what He's doing.

***

In some religions it is customary to pray for and ask forgiveness of an animal about to be slain for food. This ritual has always appealed to me. It somehow humanizes me; makes me kinder and more thoughtful. The lion takes the gazelle with no thought for his prey. The bat gobbles down hundreds of insects and thanks no one. Today I cut down a dying tree. It is now sawed up into logs for my fireplace. With each fire I light to warm my home I will give thanks to the tree and ask forgiveness. That is foolish, I suppose, but I will sleep better.

***

Over time the pantheon of gods has been reduced in numbers as discoveries have explained the previously inexplicable. No longer the Sun god, the Thunder god, the Rainbow god, the goddesses of the Seasons, the Lightening god, the goddess of Hunting, the Buffalo goddess, Neptune for the sea and Mars for victory in war. Soon there will be only one God and He for the millions of mysteries by then remaining but as yet not explained. Then Religion will regain the following it once had. And out there, somewhere, one God watches.

***

Avoid ridiculing the religious beliefs of others. Feelings on these matters are strong yet easily bruised. You will understand this best when you have had your faith derided and your philosophy mocked. Pray for universal tolerance.

***

Astrophysicists tell us that, "Our Sun is but one of hundreds of billions of stars in the Milky Way galaxy". This galaxy is disk shaped and is very thin. In proportion to its width, it is as thin as an ordinary music/video compact disc. Ours is a spiraling galaxy. Its center spins rapidly and leaves trails of matter seemingly flung outwards like a fireworks pinwheel. The Milky Way is but one of billions of galaxies which we believe comprise The Universe. This fact is simply beyond the comprehension of most of us. Our attention shifts to the woman on the beach blanket who slowly applies sun-blocking lotion to her legs.

***

A woman can bear a child about once every year, that is if she wants to get old soon and die young. A man can impregnate a woman every day or, some say, even more. Men may mate and move on while women often bear the burden of motherhood. This is certainly not fair. Is it any wonder that male dominated polygamy flourishes in Utah? What's the matter with Nature anyway?

***

The enigma of beauty is to be found in the way it is measured. Some see an object as beautiful while others see only mediocrity. Some hear an opera as art and others hear loud music and trite stories. Some stand by the hour in front of a painting in a museum while others stroll by, merely glancing. Tastes differ. We search for the companionship of those who share our aesthetic views.

***

When I reached a certain age I began to realize that my eye for a truly beautiful lady began to sharpen. I became more discerning and selective in my definition of "beauty". But at that age I also realized that the best course for me, and the best outcome for her, was for me to look at her for as long as good manners would permit and then to watch her as she moved; out of my life and on with her own. For me: "To admire no longer means desire".

***

I own many books. I have read most of them and intend to read the others and re-read the best. I intend to play the recorded music I have collected and the movies and documentaries I have lined up on shelves. I intend... That is what we old folks do that allows us to face tomorrow with determination instead of dread. We do firmly, determinedly, excitedly, intend. Tomorrow.

***

Old clothes that still fit. That's what I like to wear. Memories: a bit of the threadbare. Too many suits and shiny shoes and hated neckties have dominated my youth. They now collect dust in my closet. Old hats strewn about the house. I wear what I want and I like what I wear. I am striving at this late time in life; hurriedly struggling to become me.

***

I read in the papers that the financial situation in this country and around the world is somewhat unstable. The experts who study such things say that all will be back to normal "soon". The populace are uneasy. What people do with their money is based on emotions: typically fear and greed. An economist stated yesterday that now economics must be considered a "Behavioral Science". I think it was always so. They finally got it right.

***

No one can say how many crimes have not been committed because there are laws in existence which some have termed "too harsh".

***

Passion and Reason. Passion is unreasonable and Reason is dispassionate. Set either loose alone and man himself is lost. His life will be forfeit to the fervent, fruitless, endless pursuit of visions just beyond his grasp; of the ever receding, never satisfying, always challenging prize. He will exhaust himself. He will approach insanity and not even notice as he passes through its gate. Man's only hope is to nurture both these fraternal twins. Passion and Reason. These seemingly incompatible opposites are but symbiotic hemispheres of the brain, guiding us in our search for bliss.

***

In war the nation of Turkey is a trustworthy, ferocious ally and a horrifying foe.

***

I love France. It is Frenchmen I heartily detest. I would move my family to France except that there are so many Frenchmen there. Take away the Eiffel Tower, The Louvre, truffles and the grapes and what have you got?

***

It is the sad feature of Man that he rarely finds the right road in life until he has run low on fuel. I speak of myself here. You will be wiser, I know.

***

DROPS OF WATER, GRAINS OF SAND

Peer Pressure: When you are in the wading pool and your friends are already swimming. Or: When you are on a tricycle and everyone else is riding bicycles. Peer pressure should end sometime in your teens, else you will find yourself in deeper water than you ever imagined and riding in a police car instead of on your bike. Peers are not always right. Do not try to grow up too quickly.

***

Say a young man robs a convenience store of thirty dollars and six beers. He is caught and convicted and may get two to five years in prison. A political leader may rob a nation of sixty billion dollars, flee the country, frustrate extradition and never spend a night in any jail. Then how are we to judge or even act as members of a jury in the trial of the common thief?

***

Guns are legal, bayonets are legal, liquor is legal, gambling is legal and prescription drugs are legal. They all can kill. Why make "illegal drugs" illegal? The answer seems clear. There is big money to be made and spent on enforcing the laws against them. The growers, refiners, distributors, retailers and the graft which accompanies each and every tier of distribution; these are the impetus behind the restrictions. From the judges and the lawyers for defense and prosecution, to the array of enforcement officials in several countries, to the whore on the street, satisfying her clients, needing a few dollars to satisfy her uncontrollable habit for artificially high-priced, controlled, illegal substances; to and from all these money flows. Silly laws supported by greedy people whose tax-free grafted dollars would dry up if these drugs were to become legal. There is no mystery here; only avarice. Liquor Prohibition enacted by our grandparents is the lesson now ignored.

***

A man is rarely ready to become a father. In raising a son, each man tries to amend the mistakes made by his own father. In so doing he often omits basic lessons needed for his boy's proper development. Thus a cycle progresses; lessons taught and lessons omitted. Finally it is the son, guided by all his teachers, who must face the world and learn from his own errors. Only then is he ready to become a teacher. Only then might he make a good father.

***

The picture of a smile is not a smile. The recording of a voice is not a voice. The memory of close, warm breath is not a tender sigh. Treasure the very life of your loved one. Life is so short and death is so long.

***

A wife must be guarded and defended from him who would steal her away. Her strongest will to resist capture may finally collapse if you are not attentive. Remember, she once succumbed to your ardent campaign.

***

The caring mother of your children is forever your blessing. When you are an absent traveler, distant warrior, ex-husband or facing certain death, you are spared the anxiety of wondering about the welfare of your offspring. She is there for them.

***

"Love" is too casually used and "Adore" should be reserved for the gods.

***

Who will mourn me when I am gone? I do not know. So I mourn my dying now, while there is still time. Will I miss me? Perhaps, but I think I will not even think then. So I think now. I speak now. I dream now. I love now. I live now. I grapple with death. I am at war with my death and I carry no white flag.

***

It is a joy to watch a master craftsman at work. Be he carpenter, mason, high steelworker, or baseball player. Watch a basketball fly through the air and swish through the net; no rim. See the golfer pitch one "stony to the pin". Watch the jazzman singing through his instrument. One cannot observe for long without becoming proud to belong to the same species as these.

***

When I was introduced to her she wore a full length dress with long sleeves and a high collar. Her broad-brimmed hat and the parasol she carried shaded her from the sun. But I could clearly see her as she must have been only an hour or so before; naked in her bath, languidly sponging herself with pink soap and wondering whom she might meet this evening.

***

Babies are baptized or circumcised. Children are dogmatized. Prayers are ritualized. Martyrs die for their religion. Zealots live for their religion. Wars are instigated and sacred places pillaged in the name of religion. Yet so few are moved to spread the sacred song of God which begins and ends with the word "Love".

***

I hate nothing. I fear what I do not understand. I avoid people who cause me emotional pain or turmoil. I delay my death for as long as is practicable. I understand my enemies, (else how might I protect myself from them)? But hate? Hate is a disease which is the cancer of the psyche. Hate can kill one. Replace hate with its two-part antidote: understanding and forgiveness. I offer these with open palm and ask for them with head bowed low.

***

Fathers, do not look for gratitude from your sons. Their first home is with Mother. Then, by turns, they are nursed cuddled, coddled, taught rhymes and songs and made aware of their own curiosity about Woman. But Father is absent, tired, loud of voice, full of practicality and advice better suited to men than to boys. Father is competitor for the love of Mother. He steals both time and hugs from her and a natural resentment ensues. Father is feared; Mother is worshipped. Father and son will war. In time the boy grows up, gets married and has a family of his own. Then there is no time for talk and no inclination to establish a bond with the now aging father. The father may die and leave the script unfinished and the son unfulfilled or the two may reach the desired atonement. It is not easy to be a father or a son. Fathers and sons must learn to let time reveal their mutuality of purpose and their undeniable affection.

***

Let every grandfather live long enough to know his grandson. They are natural allies. The old man is no threat, no dreaded instructor or disciplinarian. He will not steal away with Mother. The old man is wise in the ways of games, toys, stories, jokes and has funny, old songs to sing. He feels no heavy responsibility so he lets others correct the boy and teach him the brutal lessons of life. He and the boy have fun together. Grandpa has a bright coin for the lad whether the child has been good or bad.

***

I fully expect that someday there will be a war between those who genuflect before entering a church pew and those who do not. There are many who would gladly die prosecuting such a cause.

***

Romantic love has become so confusing to me that I am at a loss as to whether to leap into the affair or to run away and hide. I wait for a sign from above.

***

The secret of success with women is a man's overcoming his fear of rejection.

***

She is too beautiful to be overlooked and too beautiful to be courted. If I won her today I would lose her tomorrow to a better man. So I hesitate, thereby assuring my loss.

***

Stay in touch with old friends. They may need you someday.

***

If a woman yields too quickly to a lover she is considered "loose". If she yields at a time too tardy she is termed "frigid". The mood for loving, if approached leisurely, usually strikes both parties simultaneously. All the rest is playacting.

***

Resist making promises. People will always remember the vows you make and never forget the ones you break. Say rather, "I will try." Then try your best.

***

If you find a question difficult to answer, ask that it be phrased differently. Perhaps then the answer will become apparent. Certainly you will have more time to craft a reasonable response.

***

When your art becomes more important to you than your income you will be on the road to becoming an artist. When your art becomes more important to you than your life you are most certain to obtain a livable income. If, instead, I am wrong and you do indeed die of starvation, well, at least you will have died a starving, young artist and not a wealthy, old bean trader.

***

Aphorisms are never meant to be taken too seriously. They are merely remnants, "out-takes" from the films of life. They are found by sweepers on the "cutting room floor" and saved as valued relics for rumination.

***

In the end we always fail to live up to the expectations of our spouses. High hopes resulting from youthful exuberance ever result in disappointments.

***

One of the problems with marriage vows is that they require each partner to "love" and "honor" the other. "Require". Therein lies the gnawing irritant. I love because I want to love and I honor all who deserve honor. Love and honor are earned allegiances and should never be required.

***

Anyone can get married and almost anyone can have children, but holding a family together is a task only for a pair of professional jugglers.

***

In flying an airplane out across an ocean to another country we seem to be defying the laws of gravity and the limits of time and distance. We might even be breaking the laws of God. A simple prayer at this time would seem to be appropriate since the act itself may be blasphemous.

***

There are many reasons not to dispute with another the existence of God. It is more important for a theist to believe than it is for you to deny. You risk undermining his carefully constructed system of beliefs upon which his entire life may be based. Should you prevail, it could prove ruinous to your counterpart. Yet you have nothing to lose by yielding. Therefore, acquiesce and move on. You will have made a friend and invested nothing.

***

Even The Catholic Church suffered a bloody schism that split it into two. I forget the matter that divided them. I think it had to do with a woman.

***

An atheist and a deist can get along perfectly as long as they avoid the subject of religion. By skirting the matter they may find that they can be the best of friends, having little else to impede their joint endeavors.

***

The formerly oppressed, when finally set loose, often bring to bear all they have learned of pain, misery and suffering, and render it threefold upon their former oppressors. The slave let loose is without mercy.

***

A single light bulb can illuminate the whole room. But a bank of floodlights cannot penetrate into the mind of the man whose eyes are shut tightly.

***

An atheist can save himself from The Inquisition simply by denying his disbelief. (He may lose his soul in which he does not believe anyway.) But a theist must die by telling the truth if his credo does not conform precisely to that of his inquisitors. Inquisitions are not fair. They are the beloved lairs of the sadist.

***

War ends in rubble, anguish, rotting bodies, moaning mothers, surrender documents and a time of antipathy resembling peace. Peace is a quiet time, hiding in silent shelters, counting its remaining children, remembering, wondering, angry, awaiting the next armed conflict. Peace is temporary.

***

I have a date with a pretty woman! How shall I dress? What shall I say? I feel like a green lad of fifteen but I am a grown man of seventy! God, help me!

***

War is a constant. War and threats of war and preparations for war and then more war. War is never concluded; it is just hiding, resting, planning, conniving, erupting like volcanoes first here, then there, then in some country of which we have never heard. There are punctuation marks called "peace", but these are an illusion. Peace is but a semicolon; a pause; a time between the wars.

***

Your Grandfather knows secrets about your father that he will never tell you.

***

For some, the magic of music seems to by-pass the ear and the mind, proceeding directly to the "heart" or "soul". These lucky few are moved by music as others might be thrilled by a rousing speech or entranced by a sublime landscape.

***

When I lost her to Death I felt the urge to follow her quickly; before she got lost in the firmament. But I heard her fading voice call back from beyond saying, "Live on! I will wait! We will have eternity together! Live on!" I wish I had not tarried here alone. I miss her so. Her voice grows faint.

***

Sometimes, when we think too much, we wonder if life is worth the toil and torment. We would do well to remember that we all have eternity to rest.

**

Since the age of primitive man, I suppose, shamans, witch doctors and priests have condemned to death the non-believer. Often not satisfied with that punishment, they then relegate him to an afterlife of everlasting, blazing torment.

**

The sacrifices made by parents are so many and great that their children cannot be expected to appreciate their magnitude till they become parents.

**

When a man attains a certain middle age he begins to worry less; about the opinion of others, about which necktie to wear, about accumulating *things*. He moves into his own center. The big decisions are behind him; have all been made. Now his loved ones are welcome but he begins to live mostly for himself. Forgive him. He has life behind him and only death ahead.

**

The urge to believe in God is so overwhelming that I wonder how a thinking person is able to resist. Why does God tempt us to doubt?

**

The sacrifices a man and wife make for each other are so many and so great that if either begins to number them the marriage will soon crumble.

**

A demanding woman makes a shrewish mate. Avoid her. A submissive woman soon engenders a painful, dreaded guilt within her husband. Flee from her. A balanced marriage is harder to sustain than a two actor play staged every night with matinees on Saturday. But it is worth it. Play on.

**

My father was harsh most of the time, until I got into trouble; personal or financial. Then he became my advocate, my mediator, my advisor, my champion and my banker. Looking back now, I think he loved me all the time but never said it and showed it only when I needed it. I wish he were alive today so that I could thank him. Can you hear me, Father?

**

Let not the atheist shun The Bible. There is more secular wisdom to be found there than in an advanced degree in the humanities.

Do not expect too much from friends. They have self-centered lives of their own to live. Rely on yourself. Be loyal to yourself. Enjoy the proximity of pals, remembering that to them you are, at best, a familiar, loyal satellite. Do they mean more to you than that?

***

The cycles of the seasons are a wonder to the youth and a signal to the aging. Each spring brings new life but the old man may become sad. He hopes for rejuvenation but will be glad just to see another winter. Does the Earth get old? Does the Earth see its certain demise? Does it care? Poor old Earth. Mother to countless events and billions of people who, each year, find renewed comfort in her bosom. Does She ever get tired? I pray not. Earth deserves a hug.

***

Act your age. People will love you for it. Mature people often form a disguise that leads them into childish games of exertion.

***

It is a rare man of advanced age who is not contentious. If you find one he has now learned that the world, with its endless cares, belongs to his sons. He listens, considers and remains silent. Unless, being much surprised, he is asked his opinion on some minor matter.

***

Attitude is crucial. Example: Your child is a costly responsibility to be fed, and clothed and educated and is always a reflection upon you. Or: A child is a gift to be nurtured, attended, encouraged, loved and empowered.

***

Setting aside matters of health, aging can be either troubling or carefree; let the elders choose. One can continue to contend with matters in the newspapers and at the local cafe, he can argue with his sons about how the world should be managed and with his wife about how the turkey should be cooked. In short, he can continue to make of his life a heated contest. Or he can relax and let the world come to him as it is, and acknowledge the diminution of his powers; the transfer of authority to his progeny. He can become an interested spectator rather than a cantankerous contestant. The choice is his.

***

There are some people who function well at nighttime. Their life begins at dusk. They know who they are: astronomers, actors, burglars, grave robbers, poachers, prostitutes and writers.

I daydream more than I used to and probably more than I should. I night dream too and I remember these dreams when I awaken. Daydreams about the way things might have been and how they may be tomorrow. Night dreams about the way my world was and what went wrong. Nightmares revealing to me my serious defects and the losses suffered by me and my loved ones therefrom. The dozing time between day and night sometimes reveals truths that have escaped me all my life. There is an informing, quiet place between sleep and wakefulness where the truth lies. We should spend more time there.

***

I dream at night about many things. I do not dream about women but I often dream about one particular woman. Out of a dozen women who might occupy my daytime thoughts there is only one who appears to me almost every night. I should wake myself but I can't. Each sad dream, it seems, must play itself out and she is always the protagonist.

***

Rules: Keep open your eyes, your ears and your mind. Open your mouth only if you can contribute something positive to the community. All behavior has its consequences. Shape your actions toward positive results.

***

Make plans. Reflect upon them. Act upon them. This simple cycle repeated can result in a meaningful, productive life. Random living is more fun, less bothersome but of little use to the subject and even less to society. Which way to live? I am still reflecting. Give me a moment.

***

I am covered over with alternate layers of arrogance and low self esteem; a dozen or more alternating zones of contradicting self-images. I used to wonder which was the real me; the self-assured egomaniac or the cowering non-entity. All my life I have endured this duality. I have finally decided to live out my life in that manner. I will change nothing. It has worked pretty well so far.

***

I own no pets. I've tried them all: dogs, cats, birds, fish and one turtle. I love them too much and they age and die; and I cry. I say let others keep pets. It is bothersome enough for me to keep me.

***

Years ago, quite by accident, I discovered a decision-making device in my pocket: a coin. Example: which road to take; the left or the right? Flip the coin: heads left, tails right. Now if the coin shows left, and you are in the least disappointed, then place the coin back into your pocket and go by the road on your right. Or if the coin shows left and you are the least bit grateful then go to the left. Either way, you, together with the disinterested advice of the coin, have decided your path. You knew before the toss but were not certain till after.

**

A girl I once loved, who dominated my thoughts and my world, one for whom I would have given my soul, has died. She was sixty-seven years old at the time of her death. I had not seen her for over fifty years. She will always be sixteen to me. Why do I find that strange?

**

Seek the advice of a friend. Visit a specialist to research your psychic history. Use an x-ray to assess a damaged bone. Rest in contemplation by a rolling seashore. Pray to God for answers. Or hold up a mirror.

> "… for the eye sees not itself,
> But by reflection, by some other things". (Shakespeare)

We wisely reach outward to discover what is inside us.

**

An epigram or a quip is often the product of hours of re-writes.

**

Her eyes seemed more than green globes to me. I saw myself therein as in a distorted mirror, somehow modified, reshaped into something better, more gentle and kind, a bit younger, perhaps, a man more to my liking. I saw past the green and the black and, I felt certain, into her soul. I, who never believed in the soul, saw her soul. I felt lost to myself and bound to her forever. "What is your name?", I asked.

**

So called "Catholic Guilt" is but a slight exaggeration of the universal guilt one feels when he knows he has done something wrong. It is just that Catholics have codified their "sins" and coupled them to consequent punishments.

**

All my life I have been very critical of myself. Yet I never seemed to improve in my behavior. I let impulse rule over logic and desire dominate prudence. This makes for an interesting existence but one filled with regret and deep sorrow. I would change many things if I could. But who of us would not? I am tired now and look forward to death as a final curtain on this play. But I would not want to miss another act if it be scheduled!

***

Some spend a lifetime finding out who they are, while others seem to be born with that knowledge. There is room on earth for both. Each may wish to be the other. Which is better? The cards are dealt. Play the cards.

***

A pilgrimage to a holy site is truly a journey into one's own spiritual realm. It is not the circling of the mosque but the pilgrim's relationship to the journey which makes him complete. A pilgrimage is all about the *trek* to Mecca or Bethlehem or The Wall and the *return* to home. The objective is but the fixed star which unerringly guides me on my journey outward and from there into my soul.

***

The advent of a privately owned recorded music library is a milestone in the journey of mankind. Thousands of musical selections rest; ready to answer my random request. Innumerable musicians sit, waiting upon my shelves, ready to perform as I demand. I will be certain never to take this boon for granted.

***

My son is often too busy to see me. This is not his choice but his set of obligations that prohibits us from enjoying a leisurely supper together. I was once that busy and declined similar invitations from my father and was absent from meals with my children. Life often interferes with living.

***

I learned more about myself in two weeks spent in a European city than I had discovered in sixty-five years in The United States. I brought those lessons home and have referred to them every day since.

***

Some of the great pleasures in life derive from simple reflection upon the past. But one needs to be selective. Remember only the good things: the happy times. We are blessed that are inclined to remember the loves and the laughter and to set aside the shame and the sadness. Else our brains would be crushed by the weight.

***

A fine film actor might enjoy a career lasting fifty years. A fine film actress is lucky to last fifteen years. Life is not fair. Or is it?

***

Another war stares at us on the near horizon. In war nothing is certain but that it will end badly; not just for the defeated but for the victors. Bodies of warriors and civilians will be interred. Sad bugle melodies will echo through the land. Torrents of tears will cascade into the valleys. Most corrupted will be the collective view of history. For it will be distorted as to cause and effect. Even actual events will be concealed and judgments on these matters will be argued for decades, the victors writing the first versions, with innumerable revisions surely to follow. Years from now the causes of this war will be totally obscured and any lessons gained from this conflict will be distorted, well concealed and forgotten but waiting to be repeated when next we confront our brother with weapon in our hand and blood in our eyes.

***

Science will always outpace the humanities. As a result, we know more about the origin of the universe than we know about what she will say when her husband is two hours late coming home from work. We know the rate of acceleration due to gravity at which, (in a vacuum), both a feather and a piano will fall simultaneously. We do not know on what day the next war will start.

***

I will not sleep well tonight. I saw her again today and I cannot rest for thinking of her. Eventually I will forget her but in the meanwhile I will lie abed and, fully awake, I will dream of moments never to come.

***

The truly creative man; the one who creates a thing which never was before and without whom this thing might have been created only much later; this man is a mutation. He is so far ahead of his time as to be considered among the insane or unfit in other ways to remain among normal men for long. It is for the rest of us to discover him and wonder; then to protect him.

Brave boys rush into battle. They are impatient for action. Then suddenly they become either dead or old. Suddenly. Their conditioning has prepared them for war and fully prepared them for the death of their comrades. Similarly, their conditioning has made them impervious to criticism of their country or to their ever having been sent into this war. It will not permit them to find this war senseless or wrong. God love the warriors and damn their obtuse leaders.

***

For years I worked in an office that overlooked a park. There were a pool and a play yard and trees and winding driveways. Children yelled, lovers strolled, and nannies pushed baby carriages. Horns honked and street vendors hailed the passersby and the site was alive with activity. I moved to the countryside where I now live. It is quiet; not much moves except the river and the treetops. I have small, wild animals and a deer or two and my writing desk. I like this life. I am happy here but I miss the old. Isn't it always like that?

***

She was young and I was as old as her father. She was beautiful and I was balding and growing wider. I was a natural teacher and she a hungry student. We loved each other till she was taught all I knew and I was imbued with a self-confidence which I had been lacking. In time we sailed away in different directions; she enlightened, I fully validated. I think of her every day. We altered each other's lives for the better.

***

Whenever I travel far from home, into another culture, I return leaving behind only a bit of currency. I always bring back trinkets of remembrance and invisible treasures for my soul. I am invigorated. I should travel more.

***

Today was bright and productive. We look to tomorrow filled with hope and ambition. But Yesterday never lets go; holding us securely and releasing us, only grudgingly, for a short time. Yesterday never lets us forget her. She wanders through our psyche, constantly crossing our path, whispering to us of long ago; of our innocence and our sins, reminding us our unfulfilled hopes and broken promises. Yesterday invades our night's dreams and shapes our daydreams and will not turn us loose. Yesterday is critical, nurturing mother to us all. Yesterday does not die till we die.

***

Farmers tumble out of bed at five a.m. or sooner. They dress, drink coffee, turn out the cattle, come back for breakfast, go out to the combine or plow, mend fences, kill a chicken, eat lunch, check the weather for tomorrow and scour the account books, hoping for a profit. Then back out into the fields to till and spray for insects. Bring in the cows. The family eats supper, they listen to the radio till nine p.m. He hugs the children goodnight and takes mom to bed. They sleep. This goes on, day after day, seven days a week till they get too old and the children take over. Year after year.

I rise at noon, loaf through brunch, read till six p.m. I snack as I read. I watch television news till about eight p.m. then nap for an hour. I rise and write till I tire. (A tired writer is a worthless writer.) I go to bed as the sun comes up; precisely as it rises on the farmer's day of toil. I will burn in Hell.

***

I am crazy. I know this because people say it is so. I know it because I laugh in all the wrong places and I cry at inappropriate times. To me it is sad when in a movie a man slips on a banana peel and falls. And it is funny when a twenty-two car pile up is shown on television. I react. Sometimes I laugh and cry simultaneously. At these times people stare at me and I look down at my feet. Perhaps I am a mirror, reflecting everything backwards. Perhaps I am a photographic negative. I don't know. I'm sorry.

***

For a short period in my life I was handsome and the ladies loved me. I was very busy. I drove a nice car and had money for necessities. I had fun, as I recall, but mostly I was overwhelmed. I never had time for myself. I was too busy chasing, capturing and then escaping. It was a frightening time. It took balding and a regular job to get me back to normal and to calm me down.

***

A "Thank You" note to God:
I am grateful for the Faith I had as a boy. I am grateful for the rigid school-ing I received at the hands of the nuns and the brothers. I am grateful for the private, secular school I attended as a lad. I am grateful for the mind that freed me from sectarian enslavement. I am grateful for the courage that sustained me through the years of family "obligation", when I lived the life of "Ought". Most of all, God, I am grateful to be alive now and to be doing what I was meant to do, (what You meant me to do), from the beginning, but was too cowardly (or brave) to undertake till my obligations were fulfilled. We lost touch, You and I. While I surely let you down many times, you never failed me. I hope we can arrange to see each other again some-time. Your pal.

***

There was a giant lion who outweighed his fellows by fifty percent. He would win all the confrontations, sire all the cubs and wrest the food from the mouths of his smaller cousins and generally wreak havoc upon the pride. How long could this situation continue? Answer: The rest of the males held a meeting and agreed to attack their larger cousin together in a well planned *coup d'etat*. They succeeded. Any single nation which becomes too powerful will finally fall victim to an alliance of the weak.

***

Solitude: The only certain place. The need to be master; finally. Be it in a mansion or a dank cave, let it be mine. Aged now, I provide my own camaraderie. The lure of women and the loyalty of children has brought me naught. They are gone. I excel now: no competitor. Though I have only a pet bird, I am master. Though no one reads my writings I am an author. Though I subsist on leaves and berries I survive. Each morning I call out to the forest, "I am awake! Be wary of me!" I listen for the echo of my voice.

***

Society is uncomfortable when it sees a man to whom it cannot affix a label. Most men accommodate society by conforming to this requisite. The maverick refuses to be classified. For this offense he is often labeled an outlaw. Yet this is a man who may change a culture to conform to his vision. In death he might become the founder of a new religion.

***

There is a special kind of pain reserved for old friends; those who have shared battles and brothels, worked side by side to raise their families, told tales, traveled together and hatched plans for "someday". The agony comes when one becomes ill and the other cannot help but only watch. Tales of old times then fall flat. What once caused laughter now brings only tears. We are aging.

***

Watch history as it plays out. Certain people are willing to sacrifice the lives of others in order to defend an "idea"; an "ideal". Not a border, not enslavement, not the annihilation of a population but a simple and easily settled dispute about a "notion". Yet leaders do not kill each other over ideas; they kill each other over property. Such wars are clothed in an "idea" and a bogus slogan posing as a "cause". Soldiers die for ideas. But for the leaders it is always greed.

***

Without your health you are like a broken machine: useless. You need urgent repair; otherwise the junk man will come by and take you away.

***

As women gain more rights for equal pay, become more powerful in business and politics, gain equality in the armed services and all other areas of the marketplace, let us watch and see how happy this makes them. Let us see how they are treated by men. Like all progressive innovations, this trend is certain to become very interesting.

***

I watch the squirrels scamper about, they chase each other and scramble for food, joust over females and provide for their young. In the evening they rest in their leafy, treetop nest. They watch us sometimes as we confront our world. They fail, as we often do, to understand us.

***

There is sadness for the man who is aging alone. Yet there is a certain gladness too: that no one cares about him. His death may be sad for him to contemplate but he is spared the sorrow of leaving mourning loved ones behind. He is spared the sight of falling tears.

***

One would think that to walk the long beach on a hot day and to see all the girls and women in their tiny bathing attire, walking or lying in languid pose; I say you might think that a man would be distracted. You would be right. But gradually having regaining my senses, I am still on the beach with my metal detector, searching for something of real value; a coin, perhaps.

***

Instrumental music needs no commentary. Unlike other forms of art it represents nothing. Music is the thing itself.

***

Twenty-five years ago I traded in friends, wives and children for the chance to be alone. I chose to acquire a large fortune and worked, isolated and tireless, to achieve that goal. Now the house, the pool, the boat and the airplane sit, polished, stocked, ready; waiting for all the strangers to arrive.

***

Alone in this hateful place, reaching for a hand and finding only a wall, I slip into total despondency. "Let me change one hour of my life!", I holler to the ceiling. "Let me go back and undo that error!", I moan. If I had thought. If I had known. I am a good man at heart. What made me do it? Years of sanity and for one hour; a vile, evil devil. Life is finished for me. Justice on Earth? Mercy on Earth? No. I await death now and nightly pray for a merciful God.

***

Necessity is the mother of religion.

***

Whenever science clashes with religious doctrine, religion loses and all who need a God doubt. But it is science who toils, perpetually seeking answers, while the faithful rest easy with their ever evolving doctrines.

***

Is there someone out there who would be cheered by a kind word from you? Then do not wait another moment. Dispatch it! Speak it now.

***

Once set upon the path of acquisition, man simply does not know when or where or how to stop. Material gain becomes a habit: an addiction. There is never enough because there is always more to acquire. He is first in a race with his neighbor and then in a more important race with himself. How can one outrun himself? He is competing with the man he was yesterday.

***

Some mornings I want to stay in bed. Yet my duty to myself says to get up, get out and begin my duty to my loved ones and to my employer. In this frame of mind I am revealing my selfishness, for I know that I cannot sleep tonight until I have fulfilled all the obligations I have heaped upon myself.

***

I have never met a saint. I have, however, met a few whom I loved more than any saint The Church ever canonized. I would happily have died in their place. Over time feelings change. Today I love almost no one. Myself perhaps but only sometimes and then with a certain suspicion.

***

The raccoons in my yard seem to have no fear of man and little respect. They eat the deer food and the squirrel food and try their best to get at the people food that ends up in the garbage bin out by the shed. At dawn, when their foraging is nearly complete, I see them on my porch, picking at the bird seed spilled upon the deck. We exchange glances. I offer them an obscene gesture which they ignore. I laugh at their indifference. Then we retire; they to their hiding place and me to mine.

***

The Catholic school which I attended provided me with the best education available. I learned things there that have served me well for over sixty years. Still it left out the happy things and intimidated me with dogma and fear for my own afterlife: my soul. They educated me for life but made me afraid to live it.

***

God the Father always has time to listen to our prayers. He always answers them. It is our task to hear and interpret His often obscure responses.

***

To some, arguments are considered fractious. To others they are but intellectual exercises. To still others they are cause for the dissolution of a friendship. To the lucky few, these heated discussions create a lasting bond between coequals who together seek Truth.

***

Movies are a weakness with me. They are my novels. Some I watch several times and a few I see more often. I am a critical man and have walked out on many films I thought were designed for morons or the sexually depraved. But if I am absent from home for long or if you see the flickering light of my television at odd hours, you can bet I am watching a movie or two. I learn more about Man from films than I could from simply living. The heroes and villains on film are blatant, while in life so much is hidden from us. Where in life can we find a good morality tale? By the time the newspapers and the lawyers and the TV preachers are done with me, I am hard-pressed to discern the good guys from the bad. Some go to church; I go to the movies.

***

Some people are non-stop talkers: loquacious. Others are closed-mouthed thinkers: taciturn . I trust neither. I do not know what either really thinks.

***

Name one conformist whose name appears in one history book.

***

The future is well planned yet unknown. The past is partially obscured by time and written under the influence of selective memory. The present is known to each of us only through the prism of our unique viewpoint or bias. The Truth is an apparition. It changes with one's perspective. It is subject to endless interpretation, reflection, its degree of absolutism and its place on the scale of time. As we pursue it, Truth runs far ahead of us. We can watch as it becomes smaller and smaller till it disappears into myth. Truth will forever remain subjective.

***

Many wars are like marital quarrels. By the time they are over there remains only the question of how they got stated.

***

Two men should never quarrel in front of one or more women. From deep inside the subconscious of each man emerges the primordial set of base emotions. He must display his manhood. He must prove to be the stronger of the two; a fit instrument for procreation. He must use every means to appear the dominant one. Testosterone and adrenaline drive the encounter. Hell can break loose. Take away the woman and the dispute might well be settled with the toss of a coin, a handshake and a mutual toast.

***

A young athlete can remember every game he ever lost. He can recall with exquisite accuracy each important game he ever won; with scores and highlights. The old man remembers the smells of the air, the camaraderie of his team and the skill of their opponents; the nobility of the game. When old men play golf, they do not play to win so much as they play to play.

***

Again we are on the verge of war. While historians debate the causes of almost every war in which The United States has been involved (and fail to reach a consensus), we prepare for still another slaughter. Perhaps the best explanation is to be found in the nature of man himself. Old men send young men to war. The economy expands, the rich get richer and the competition for women tilts in favor of the survivors; the fittest. Overdrawn cynicism? I will listen attentively to your explanation.

***

Morning doves forage together in pairs. I cannot tell the male from the female but they can. When you see one you can bet you will soon see the other. They mate for life: "till one of them dies", it is said. They are peaceful and when I watch them I am at peace. They are feathered marriage counselors. What dour chaplain performed their nuptial ceremony?

**

At the casino, do not play Keno, slot machines or roulette. Your only hope to win is at blackjack (21) or craps. These two games are very hard to learn properly and even then the odds are slightly against you. You want to walk out with their money in your pocket? Then get ahead and quit. Getting ahead is much easier than quitting. It takes character to walk away a winner.

**

What is the point of solitaire? I used to watch my mother play. She taught me the games. My father viewed solitaire as a prodigal waste of time. In the middle again, I learned the games and played some when I was alone. A deck of cards and a flat surface can keep the mind sharp and the nerves quiet. There are lessons to be learned: patience, mathematical odds, timely risk, certain tactical skills, respect for "lady luck", composure when losing and a tolerance for loneliness.

**

Life is worry, sorrow, fear, pain, disappointments and a series of unfulfilled dreams. Life is agony and you only get to live it once.

**

Listening to serious music is a solitary endeavor. In a thousand seat hall, one is alone with the performance. Artist/composer are one and there is you. When things work well, I begin to undergo a sort of religious experience. I attend too few concerts these days. I will return.

**

As a child I was lucky. I had a productive father, a loving mother and two older sisters who watched over me. I was raised by three women and provided for by a strong man. The Catholic church, the Nuns and the Brothers were my spiritual instructors. All was well for a time and then came Life. I was never prepared for the ensuing struggle. No one ever told me it would be like this.

**

The Boy Scout pace consists of running fifty steps and then walking fifty steps. Alternating this routine one can cover a lot of real estate before tiring. Life itself was like that for me. I worked hard and played hard and sometimes I would forget to sleep. Now I sleep for several hours and doze for several more. The Senior Scout Pace. When I tire from sleeping and dozing, I get busy playing.

***

What is to become of the recently paroled felon? What has prison done for him? What has prison done to him? Who is he now? Only those whom he knew before his incarceration will care for him now. Will it be a loving family or his old crew? He will choose. God, guide and protect the bewildered parolee.

***

On the edge of war everyone is on edge. Peace demonstrations are matched by war marches. Then there are the small pockets of those who pray for the safety of their soldiers. When the shooting begins the alignments will change. Each nation involved will, as one, pray for victory, for the destruction of the enemy and the safety for their own troops. Years after the shooting stops, there will be memorials for those who died. Former adversaries will meet to select their new, mutual enemy and make their plans for battle.

***

An unexpected, greeting message from a misplaced friend can turn one's day around. It can turn a life around. Out there, someplace, an old friend of yours sits wondering. His life seems dreary. He awaits something; he knows not what. A note or call from you might change his day; his life. Are you too busy?

***

When the Japanese play jazz, their perfect execution of their instruments, while to be expected, never ceases to amaze the audience. The groups I heard in Tokyo almost made me believe that Jazz was born in that town over a hundred years ago. Remember Pearl Harbor? Peace sure beats the hell out of war.

***

We all love our spouses and our children and believe that they love us. Speaking the words reinforces the feelings. Saying "I love you" makes the truth more true. We never tire of being loved. We never tire of hearing it. Speak it today and see the smile. Hear it today and feel the warmth.

***

There is some music played at "concerts" which takes on the character of the staging, the costuming, the ambient lighting and the audience participation in the festivities. Such an event is a spectacle rather than a concert. Afterward there is an element of . "Did you see… ?" rather than, "Did you hear… ?" Theater requires many accouterments. Music stands alone.

***

For decades I was a strident atheist. Then something happened to me. Something happened to her. She died. Like waves from the ocean, memories and dreams of my own religious childhood came rushing at me, swirling about my legs and thrusting me backwards; wave after wave; day after day. I came to accept her death only by believing her to be safely in Heaven. I ache to see her again there. I now believe I will.

***

I still read John Steinbeck. "The Grapes of Wrath", "Of Mice and Men" and his short stories and short novels. "Cannery Row" draws me back time and again. Steinbeck is able to imbue these "unsavory characters" with a nobility that revealed the writer more than the characters. In seeing and reporting and describing these folk to us, he showed us how to empathize with poverty, determination, hopefulness and a faith in tomorrow without which none of us can live for long. In reading about people who eat canned beans three times a day, I was able to look at myself and be glad that I was a member of the same species. We are all poverty stricken in a way and all full of hope. None of us has all he wants. We are in pain yet we go on. Some appear to have no reason to live yet still struggle. We know the joy of simply surviving. We all are citizens of Cannery Row and Steinbeck knew it.

***

I remember the sights and sounds of the lake. Boaters, fishermen and water skiers by day and frogs, firelies, loons and crickets by night. Sometimes we slept in the boat, moored by the pier. The rolling water rocked us into wonderland. We dreamed beneath the mosquito net. The boat rubbed the pier and we incorporated that sound into our dreams. The boat, the sounds and she are all gone now and I dream of nothing. I drove by the lake only once since then. It was crowded with strangers; like the rest of my life.

***

If a man is not of two minds on any serious question, he needs to re-think the matter.

***

The President says it is time to go to war. So we will go. We live in a democracy but sometimes we act like we are the subjects of a dictator. Mostly we do as we are told. Our occasional protests are heard, tolerated and then ignored. We vote for those whom we distrust the least. We hope for a better leader but we settle for what we get. Someday there will come a leader who…

***

The best time of the day for me is the nighttime. I crawl beneath the covers and I think of the day just past. Then I wonder about tomorrow and then, suddenly I awake and tomorrow has become today.

***

To the warrior, war itself is preferable to the terror of waiting for battle.

***

I was ten years old. My aunt was the most beautiful woman I had ever met. I had dreams about her. She was full figured and full of life and laughs and smelled like a beauty parlor. With red hair and green eyes and she looked like a grown-up ought to look. It was explained to me that I could never marry my aunt, so I vowed I would marry her double. At twenty I married someone of my own age who was even more beautiful. And she loved me! Life is smarter than those who live it.

***

The snow is melting. The chipmunks have stirred from their winter hiding place to vie with the birds for the sunflower seeds. Basketball tournaments are in full swing. Ducks are on the river again and I saw a convertible automobile with the top down just yesterday. Soon the lush greenery will appear; and then Easter. My country embarks upon a new war on Wednesday.

***

The position of the sun tells me the day is waning. But there is still the still of the night to come; the quiet time that lets my mind loose from the mundane and lets me launch myself into reverie. Selfish man, I will light the room, scan a book or two, gather my writing tools and open the flood gates. What will pour through I do not know but it will be mine: of me. For too long I have been an instrument of others. At night I implement me.

***

I gave up on women years ago. I know that for some men a woman is a necessity; that for others she is the object of a perpetual pursuit. To these men I tip my hat and bid, "congratulations" and "good hunting!". As for me, the hunt was exciting, the capture quite blissful… for a time. Then I and my prey became bored, it seemed. So off we went in search of other climes and other captures. One day I began to think of other things and I judged the chase to be occupying an inordinate amount of my time. Now I write and, while there is no one to read my words, I am content to have no responsibilities. I lack the ability to commit to anyone but dedicate my life to whomsoever might read what I write. I am alone without being lonely and a solo who is not a solitary.

***

Thursday, March 18th: So far, the war goes well for my country. The prices of oil and gold are dropping on the Mercantile Market. I will pay less now for gasoline and my dollar will buy more gold. All is well.

***

The stock market can bring on good fortune, frustration and/or failure but it is rarely boring. Like the casino, it is never dull. But this week I witnessed an event not seen by my before but, I was told, it is not unique in the history of the securities business. A war has begun. This was a war which had been discussed but was not assured. Now that it is underway my stocks rise; I make unearned income while strong, young soldiers forfeit their lives. This is unsettling to me. At the tavern my fellow investors rejoice while I silently toast those honored dead. Something is the matter with me. Perhaps I should drink faster. No. I'll leave now and return to the tavern later; when I have thought this through. There is more than money to be considered here.

***

All wars have a duration; a date of start and a date of cessation of hostilities. But all wars began long before outright hostilities and they end, if ever, only years after the last drop of blood has been shed.

***

War is the direct result of the failure of leaders to settle differences peacefully. They assemble generals whose warriors dutifully execute plans and follow orders. (Soldiers fight for reasons they often do not fully understand.) Innocent, nameless civilians, whose leaders pose as protectors, are ground up in the machinery of war. The war ends and the dead are buried in their graves. State leaders and their generals retire to sunny climes.

***

In Baghdad the bombs fall. Terror is nationwide in Iraq. Via orbiting satellites, images of the war are directed onto the television set in my kitchen. I pour a second cup of coffee and make plans to go shopping.

***

The strategy of my country is to produce "shock and awe" in the minds of our adversaries so as to demoralize them; press them into an early surrender. I am horribly shocked and in awe. I surrender.

***

For a man to think clearly he must first put far from his mind any idea that springs from or leads toward religion. Life is a practical matter.

***

Money is a tool. Like a hammer, it can be used to mend a fence or crack open a walnut. Like a firearm, it may help feed your family or slay your enemy. Use all tools carefully.

***

The need to reproduce one's kind is universal. This is natural. Only in humans is this instinct so regulated, convoluted and controlled by custom. Only by humans are all its self-imposed rules so regularly disregarded.

***

If I should fall in love with a married woman what is to be done? Should I bid my heart be still? Should she loudly spurn my attentions? Should her husband intercede with a caution or a saber? I know how lions and gazelles react; but what about humans? The answer: avoid married women.

***

On the subject of women there is only one proven rule and it is almost never obeyed. Avoid all attractive women. That is unless you are ready to sacrifice your life to her and to your children and to your grandchildren and have your heart broken a dozen times by those whom you love and break the heart of one or more of these. I repeat: "Oh, what a tangled web we weave when first we fashion to conceive".

***

We search for perfect love: for a partner, a protector, an advisor we can trust. We seek direction on this confounding road. In this world of moral ambiguity we need a compass. He or she is there, waiting for you to call.

***

Death: the slight toll paid at the end of the ride. The petty price for living.

***

At an advanced age I now have the time and the hindsight to study my past. It seems to me that I am now about where I wanted to be all my life. It is as though every step I took from the moment I was born has led me to this place; the place I wanted to be all along. Stride forward, young friend. You are on a winding road, rolling over steep hills and into dimly lit valleys but a road that will lead you unerringly to home. Keep moving.

***

They tell me I will recover. The pain will slowly subside, they say. Time and patience will heal, they assure. But they are wrong. She is gone forever and I must daily resist the urge to follow her. Or I might strive to become another Orpheus and play the lyre and sing her back to my side.

***

Hello, there. I am an old candle. Now, as you see, only a flickering taper. I soon will be burned out; a scorched wick in a small, dry pool of spilled tallow. An eternity of darkness awaits me. Yet I leave behind billions of brightnesses! Once I helped to illuminate a whole cathedral! I then added lustrous radiance to a lighthouse lamp; then warmth to a bedroom. Once I stood for one whole night, lit in a window, and brought in from the snow-storm my lady's lost husband safe and sound. I never injured anyone. I lived well. Who could help but be envious of my life?

***

He who seeks to study life has much to learn. Like any drama, it has a beginning, a middle and an ending. Some say there is yet another segment but they are not reflecting upon life. They are contemplating afterlife.

***

The boy was eighteen years old. He had finished his secondary education and planned to go further with his learning. His skill at mathematics boded well for a degree in engineering. He joined the army and hoped to gain his education while attending school therein. At twenty and well on his way to his goal, he was called to keep his part of his bargain with the military. He was a good boy and pleasant and smart as could be. He was a fine soldier and will be missed.

***

DROPS OF WATER, GRAINS OF SAND

Each step forward in the life sciences confronts us with a moral problem. Should we utilize the new? Does it lead to yet another moral dilemma? There is one set of certainties: a) knowledge will grow and create new problems; b) people will choose to grow or choose not to.

***

It is easy to get a law passed that secures the modes of today and yesterday. Try to convince Congress that a law is needed in anticipation of tomorrow's problems and they scurry for safety into the open arms of the past.

***

We can imagine sights seen long ago. We can call to memory the sounds of the gurgling creek . We can picture the face of our absent loved one. We can hum an old song and never miss a note. Yet we can never remember that which we have smelled. We can *recognize* odors but never *recall* them. They must be experienced anew each time. No one ever dreamed an aroma.

***

A nation can rewrite history for only so long; then History begins to write itself. The truth remembered and memories passed from father to son live longer than any history book.

***

Ethnic jokes are as old as humor. The best of these are told by the members of the group at which they are aimed. Examples of this irony abound. An ethnic joke thinly disguises tolerance, compassion and love.

***

For proof of God, one must spend his whole life searching. For proof of the need for God, one has only to look within himself for one brief moment.

***

A shrinking middle class is the first signal of the eclipse of any country. The tax base disappears. The poor outnumber the middle class which can no longer support the prosperous. The wealthy have won the game and lost the nation. The straw house falls.

***

Sometimes, when I compose, I fall in love with my words. I think that anyone who will not revere my writings must surely be an idiot. This attitude is dangerous, egotistical and an error most foolish. It is wrong.

***

A retired man should learn to perform the tasks which have heretofore been the province of hired tradesmen. He will thus stimulate his mind and exercise his body. He will save his money and reinforce his pride.

***

A man is never alone when he reads. He is in direct connection with the author. I read biographies. My friend prefers novels and others study history. Most books are written by serious people who offer up new ideas to be accepted, rejected or merely contemplated. Your library awaits you.

***

The most favored seats at the theater, the ballpark and in the church are reserved for the wealthy.

***

Every simple food I was taught to love as a child has remained my favorite. Sixty years later I live alone and can eat all those simple things Mother and I concocted in our yellow kitchen. But my doctor says that diet will kill me. He says I must cut out most of my favorite foods or die.
"To be or not to be."

***

My close pal of fifty years has lost all his money in bad investments. He needs help. I have money put away for medical care; to be needed someday. I will not lend or give money to my friend. I must be selfish. Life is cruel and only the cruel survive. I am satisfied. Then why do I feel so guilty?

***

I saw another one today; in the grocery. A raven hair beauty dressed in black slacks with a black sweater. I looked at her only long enough to see the blue-green eyes and full red lips. She smiled. I smiled back and quickly left the store having forgotten why I came in. That was too close.

***

Both of my ex-wives independently determined that I am a misogynist. This is just not true. I simply do not like talking to or listening to women. We share almost no common ground and I already have enough children.

***

As a youngster I used to pray for many things. Some prayers were answered with things and others were answered with silence. Today the only prayers I say are prayers of thanks. I have had enough good fortune for any three men. Thanks, God. You took care of me even when I forgot to pray.

***

Flaming love is suitable for the young and for procreation. Cool love is for the busy parents. Warm love is for the mellow years; relaxed, spontaneous, enjoyable and merely part of sweet devotion.

***

I met a stranger today. It is rare for me to meet anyone new. I am more comfortable with old friends. But today I had a great time talking and laughing and trading stories with the stranger. Maybe we will meet again. Every day something exciting might happen.

***

Living within a society is a taxing business and devours valuable time. Associations require attention. We must relate to relatives and submit to the "Do's" and "Do Not's" required by the marketplace. Better to be alone and let the law of the lonely house be the only law of the land.

***

I used to fish often, long ago, when I lived on a lake. I could catch a meal for us within an hour. Now I live on a river; high above the river. I am too lazy to walk the stairs just to fish. And if I were to cast my fly rod, the line would be caught in the overhanging trees. I am too lazy to clean any fish I might catch. And no one can cook a fish like my ex-wife. The fat trout can swim easy now; free from fear. Their once ferocious predator has worn himself out.

***

There are movie stars and there are actors. A performer may be either and, if luck is with him, he may earn a good living. A performer may be both a "star" *and* an "actor". If so, he will be honored beyond the dreams of kings. He will be coveted by the masses and praised by his peers. He will have sought neither money nor praise but merely forever to become another person, time after time, on stage or screen: forever to become another; until his death.

***

Is time my master or my slave? What is time? A wise man said, "One minute is not very long when your girlfriend is sitting on your lap but it is a very long time when you are sitting on a hot stove". So structure your life that it results in pleasant activities. Let your work be an expression of your will; not a chore you do in exchange for money. Doctors tell us we will live longer if we are happy. Time may then fly by and we might die sooner than we had wished but we will have lived longer than we had ever hoped.

Late at night, with the world outside silent in sleep, I, like the owl or raccoon, go hunting. I hunt for words. I dig up synonyms, pounce on ideas, juggle phrases, and polish paragraphs. Some nights are fruitless rummages and I come to bed in the morning tired and defeated. I worry about the nocturnal hunters and their new, spring young. Their toil is a nightly necessity. They do their duty without complaint. Their kind have survived out there since that stately walnut tree was but a sapling. My writing is done in the warmth and shelter of a house. My "task" is merely self-indulgent whimsy. In the end my vanity pales before their courage. Sometimes I am embarrassed to be me.

At this time in my life I am beginning to lose old friends to death. Old friends are irreplaceable. It is they with whom I shared youthful adventures, foolish pranks and hopeful dreams for the future. But now the hopes of youth and future have become merely ideas wasting away in some old, unused segment of my mind. Memory dominates my thoughts and every remembrance includes one or two loved ones now "gone before". Memories are all there is for me. Place them beside "reality" and both suffer by comparison. Yesterday is gone and today is full of both regret and yearning for the past. I read a poem long ago that expressed the wish that the poet himself might die like an exploding rocket in the night; flashing brightly for a moment and then fading into darkness. Being human and old is punishment enough. There is no need for Hell.

It is a fact that 98% of the time men and women are in complete control of their actions. It is that other 2% that makes newspaper headlines.

In an airliner I fly over the ocean. It is a bright, clear day and I have a window seat. Today I look out at the lush blue water far below. It seems clear as the brilliant blue sky above. Then I see the pinpoint of a boat and a larger, glistening, white wake that fans out wide in the water: so far down there yet visible to me. I see two white tails following some moving thing. Then I visualize a man like me, looking up from that boat into the smooth, blue sky and gazing at the two white streaks that fan out wide behind my craft; the vapor trails. We both travel upon the blue, leaving behind twin white markers; signaling to each other that all is well.

One of the most closely held secrets of the fine actor is that he would do his work for nothing. The pleasure is in the doing and the reward is in the applause. This peculiarity differentiates him from the producer who, without "front" money, would not even exist. Money and art make uneasy partners.

***

When one forgets to shave, to change to fresh undergarments, to make up his bed, to take out the trash, to call on his friends or contact his relatives; these together can be taken as a sign. He is either about to announce a scientific discovery, submit a manuscript for publication or commit suicide.

***

Some artists bloom early and constantly. Some grow fast, burst into glorious blossom and fade. Some seeds lie underground for many years then, as if awakened from a coma, burst forth and become handsome, flowering trees. Art erupts unexpected in forms unfamiliar, often from the people least likely.

***

In plane and solid geometry classes I learned how to compute the area of an equilateral pentagon and the volume of a sphere. I was tested and I qualified. I am seventy years old and I have never had occasion again to use these formulae. I was taught how to father by watching my father. Right or wrong, I used what I learned for twenty years. Schools should teach parenting.

***

All that we can teach our children is the accumulation of all that we know. As children ourselves we were instructed to learn all we could in order to become qualified for a job that would provide income to raise our own family. We taught our children likewise. What about the stars and the oceans and the faces in the clouds? What should we teach about the families from which we blossomed? How do we learn to deserve a hug or to give one even when not deserved? The school building encloses but a small portion of learning.

***

If a man is not of two minds on any serious question, he needs to re-think the matter.

***

For years there was the same photograph of me on each of my mother's successive pianos. I am pictured in a sailor suit, hatless and holding a bright, striped, rubber ball and smiling as though I were holding the world in my arms. I was four years old when the picture was taken (1938) and fifty-five when she died and it was removed. She once told me that the ball was given to me by the photographer to hold so that I would smile and that it was returned to its rightful owner only seconds after a satisfactory photo was executed. She recalled that I cried all the way home as she tried to explain that the ball did not belong to me but to the man with the camera. I remained implacable for hours, she said. One day, in the 1960's, I was in the music room of her large home, listening to her play, and I glanced at the photo. I asked her why she did not simply give the man a dollar for the ball and let me have it? She stopped playing and looked at me, tears welling in her eyes, "Jimmy, I did not have a dollar. After paying the photographer, I had five cents left for my bus fare home and you rode for free and that was all there was."

***

When do we grow up? When do we cease to need our parents? When do we discard our heritage? When we pay less attention to the welfare of our parents and more to ourselves we are teaching our children a lesson they are apt to remember. Let the love travel up and down the family line.

***

I found an old photograph the other day; forty years old. It depicted my then wife, more beautiful than I had remembered her, our five year old son and our three year old daughter holding her rag doll. My wife and I divorced after twenty-eight years of marriage. Our daughter died. The beautiful lady and our son and I simply aged. Sometimes I hate old photographs.

***

If I had my life to live over I promise I would work harder, drink less alcohol, save more money and pay attention to serious matters. But I do not have to keep that resolution, do I?

***

Life is a game of solitaire. We like very much to win, but it is the challenge of the game well played that keeps us coming back to the board.

***

The older I become the more I understand my once unscrutable, late father. We are more alike than I had thought.

***

When I was a lad of eighteen years or so, my mother purchased a lovely family of delicate porcelain chickens. There were a rooster, a hen and three chicks; (as my family had a father, a mother and three children). She arranged them on the fireplace mantle with the male and female facing each other; hovering over the three chicks in between. The parents coequal, protecting their young, I suppose. When my father came home, Mom showed him her new purchase. He appeared to admire the grouping but suggested an alteration in the positioning of the family. He placed the rooster in front, the hen close behind and the chicks lined up at the rear; in a marching column. Mother was aghast! "No you don't, Clifford"!, she scolded. I covered my laugh with a cough. She set the grouping back to her liking. Every few months Dad would re-arrange the chickens his way. He would invariably execute this blasphemy at night, after coming home late from a political function. Mom would correct the error as soon as she noticed it and there was never another word spoken about the on-going, sporadic war. This struggle was either very funny or very serious: I was never sure. After my parents died, the family of chickens dispersed; one or two now reside in another state.

"Love does not consist in gazing at each other, but in looking outward together in the same direction." — Antoine de Saint-Exupéry

***

I have never met anyone who did not claim to "love" music. But I know many who cannot carry a tune, own no recordings, hum or whistle no tunes nor voluntarily attend any concerts. Yet they love music! Why will people never admit even to being indifferent to music? I love music.

***

The first law of life is to have faith in yourself. The first duty of a parent is to instill learning and discipline in a child so that he may become self-confident. Belief in one's self must precede all other faith, else we are slaves to the teachings of others; to the preaching of any passing prophet.

***

We are the stronger but the enemy defends its home. Military historians state that on a neutral field of battle it is preferable to have a two to one military advantage over your enemy. In their home territory a six to one advantage is preferred. Yes, men fight harder when they are defending their homes and families than they do when invading another's homeland. The Russians, during World War II, defended Stalingrad (1942-1943) for many months, during the Russian winter, surviving on rats and human flesh. The invading Germans finally gave up and went home having suffered 300,000 casualties. So more Americans are needed for this battle. They are coming.

***

Be careful of a man with ideas who is not afraid to die for a cause in which he believes. Though he may indeed die, his death will serve as a call to others of like mind, perhaps to throngs, who may take up his banner and spread upheaval throughout the land. Be careful of ideas. They often outlive the man.

***

In the three major Biblical religions we learn it is not enough to live by The Ten Commandments; one must believe that they were given to us by a personal God. The Commandments make common sense. Belief in a personal God requires imagination and faith in the unknowable.

***

Freshly bathed and shaved, I leave now for the grocery. My want list is short these days. But I may get to see the dark-haired checkout girl who always smiles at me and waves, as though I were important!

***

Suicide bombers and suicide pilots readily give their lives in the name of a cause they believe to be greater than themselves. They are fanatics. Irrational zeal can paralyze a nation and cause unforeseen international consequences. To kill all fanatics is impracticable. (For every one slain, two will rise.) Rather search out their grievances and seek redress. While I will not yield to violence or threats of violence, I will talk and work peacefully to settle matters of dispute.

***

Having taken an early retirement, I now notice that every living creature is busier than I have ever noticed them to be. The grasshopper, the hawk, the chipmunk, the mailman, the shopkeeper are all buzzing about, flitting from here to there, all with important things to do. Every car in town is on the streets I think. Was I once a part of this mass motion? Well, no more. I eat and sleep, I play my music and read my books. I peck at the writing machine and I daydream. I should have been doing more of these things when I was younger.

***

I have no respect for a politician who avoids controversy. Hi is doing little for his constituency and interested in only getting re-elected. He strives to offend no one. He yearns to survive in a static world where tomorrow brings no surprises.

DROPS OF WATER, GRAINS OF SAND

I browse through old photographs, studying faces and remembering places and things I did and who was there and what was said and who is dead. It is not a pleasant task, sorting out the old and assigning each item to an heir. But, my father taught me: "Do the distasteful things early in the day so that the rest of the time can be enjoyable". These photos make me smile and cry simultaneously. They represent good times gone. There is little joy in seeing my children as they were at three and five. There is just reality, telling me I'm old now since the time has gone. (*a la* Ira Gershwin)

***

War has an extensive prologue, a tumultuous and melancholy script and a tragic epilogue which is often the prologue to yet another, violent play.

***

On September 11, 2001 an attack occurred in New York City wherein 3000 people were killed by the purposeful crashing of two airliners into the World Trade Center towers and then a single attack by one airliner into the Pentagon in Washington D. C. On March 31, 2003 a governmental commission was convened to seek means of preventing such attacks in the future. In the meantime The United States has responded with wars in Afghanistan and even now in Iraq. The wheels of government grind slowly; if at all.

***

To study and understand a particular religion is not nearly so difficult as to try to live by the precepts of that faith.

***

It seems easier today to mount a war between nations than to arrange serious dialogues. Shoot first: talk later.

***

In passion there is physical abandon. In romantic love it is the ego that is lost. When the two events are combined, the bonding is secure.

***

We are sailing in the middle of a large, inland lake. A black storm cloud roars in from the west. Should we try for the trip back into the storm, towards home, or let the wind blow us toward the distant, unfamiliar shore? Listen to the chant of the winning politician. Put the wind at your back. Wherever it takes you, go with the wind, amigo. Go with the wind.

***

Why do we visit cemeteries? Do we really want to re-visit the past? The past is but an anvil we drag behind us. It reminds us of what we were and slows us in the urgent process of becoming. Leave the dead alone.

***

I met her half a lifetime ago. For three weeks we frolicked in Nice. I've not seen her since. There is a photograph of her I took then and keep today. Knowing that we both have changed so much and that the memories will sadden me, I look at the picture only sometime in summer and I remember. Even now the sight of her smiling image and my recollections are well worth the pain of loss.

***

Who will know if I steal this thing tonight? By tomorrow morning I will be in Oregon and who is to say I've not been there for a week? The owner of this will not miss it for some time; perhaps never. I do not really need it; I just want it. More exactly I just want to steal it. I think these things just before I walk back toward my motor home; empty handed. What's the point, I wonder. What I really want is to have effect. There are other ways to be noticed. I could write something that others might read. And stealing is a hard habit to break.

***

It was late at night and I was on a lonely duty: a border guard. An old man limped toward my post from within the neutral section. Trembling, he was without papers but pleaded to pass. He was going into the fight, he stated; into the combat zone. "Over there is my home", he indicated with quivering hand. "Years ago I ran away to escape the oppression but now we are invaded. My place is in the battle". I searched him thoroughly. He carried no weapons but said he felt certain he would find a rifle or saber or dagger or sharp stone along the way. It was my duty to refuse him passage but I saluted him smartly and let him cross. He hobbled off into the darkness of the desert. I knew that he would battle bravely if given the chance. I hoped that when he died he would suffer no pain. I am ashamed that I failed in my duty to turn him back, but I am not sorry.

***

When I have cannon and rifles, while you have only bows and arrows, the outcome of the battle can be predicted with near certainty.

***

Gambling with cards is neither wise nor stupid. Simply know the game and play for reasonable stakes. Quit when you are ahead. Otherwise don't play.

**

The law is no protection against those who have no respect for the law.

**

If Man is a reasoning animal then why, tell me, does he so often act without reason? Answer: Because Man is also a creature of passion, rage, war, envy, avarice, base desires, and golf. I play computer games.

**

God loves us in spite of our faults. Who else would? Therefore, God exists.

**

From a fictitious father.
My grandfather fought in The Spanish-American War. My uncle died in France in 1918. My father served in World War II and I figured it was my turn. I went to Korea in 1952. I remember the hills and the battle cries of the enemy. I remember the rats and the cold. I made it through without a scratch. Our only child died the in the jungle in Laos in 1973 and our government did not acknowledge his heroism till just a few years ago. Now there is war in Iraq and another just finished in Afghanistan. I am too old to go and Anna and I have no one else to send. God, bless America!

**

Friday afternoons, after work, used to signal the beginning of the restful weekend. A time for gaiety, gossip and beer. To me, now a retired man in his sixties, they have no special meaning. Yet I like to go to the bar on Friday night and listen to the foolishness the youngsters spout; about the ball games and the workplace, the women and the cars. This I do and wish that I were one of them; to be part of the patter.

**

"Man is a reasoning animal", so they say. That's our problem. We weigh too many factors before we decide. We wait too long to act. We suppress our instincts as we puzzle out our plans. Then we are as likely as not to get it wrong. We have the power to destroy our planet but we bicker with our neighbor as to how to "worship". We murder each another for dozens of motives. We kill ourselves for no apparent reason. We war with other nations for reasons our leaders disguise and which we do not understand. The victors falsify history to suit their needs, and we ask, "How did this all begin?"

**

JAMES C. COURTNEY

87

Food, clothing and shelter are all we need. Add a partner, a weapon, a tool or two and we can live a good life. But few of us are satisfied till we own a hilltop house in Malibu. We "reason" our way past need to greed. So fulfillment eludes us as we relentlessly pursue "more". The animals in my back yard have God's plan figured out. What's the matter with us?

***

If my dad were alive today he would be proud of me, I think. But, knowing him, he would not tell me so. It seems to me that I sought his approval all my life; without success. He thought his job was to provide for me and my sisters and to improve me. Love and hugs and praise were my mother's tasks. Once, toward the end of his long life, I phoned him at his home, hundreds of miles away. He was alone in the house, since my mother had died a year before. At the end of the conversation I said the words to him I do not remember ever having said before. "And Dad, remember; I love you." There was a pause. Then, his voice in a whisper as though someone might overhear, he responded: "Same from my end." That was his first and only attempt at intimacy and it was plenty good enough for me.

***

Hindsight is cold and cruel and always too late. It rests astride the words, "If only". Hindsight can be a brutal monster when we visit a stone in the cemetery. I do not want to know about tomorrow.

***

Every man should, at least once in his life, win a prize by the action of pure skill. Every man should, at least once in his life, win a prize by the action of pure luck. He will then be confident that skill and luck will win him the world. Lady Luck dances with all. Much skill is required in order to take full advantage of good fortune. Learn the game and dance with the Lady.

***

Before war begins the Foreign Policy Ministers are critically involved in the nation's affairs. Their task is to preserve peace through negotiations. After war is under way, these give way to The War Department and their voices are muted. After the chaotic battles cease, all heads turn back to the peace seekers. They are expected to recapture order: to pick up the pieces.

***

When my friend agrees with me, he is being reasonable. When he contradicts me he is being both unreasonable and disagreeable. Yet friends must be tolerated.

***

The war goes very well. The humanitarian crisis escalates: the rescue of the displaced and hungry, the threat of disease. The survivors cry for food, clothing, shelter and clean water. Our army claims victory. The newly liberated populace cheers our soldiers. Now is a time for Nation building. We plan to create a democracy in a country which is surrounded by a region of the world ruled by a group of autocratic theocracies. We are told that peace is at hand.

***

First the beautiful woman. Then the fury of courtship and the pageantry of the wedding. Then the passion and the new, strange games. Then the children and the home and the garden and the fence and each day becomes another link in a burdensome chain. Yet we remain. Perhaps it is in the nature of man that he transform himself from a stately stag into a beast of burden and she from a shy doe into a brood mare. I hope not; but I fear.

***

Our sons are first too young to listen to our lessons and then too busy, then too preoccupied with their own lives and then, when they are finally ready, we fathers die. Thus ignorance thrives and sad histories are repeated.

***

When old friends die we are, by degrees, left more lonely. They seem to fall like the objects in O. Henry's "The Last Leaf" and, it seems that only we are left. We grow more lonely and leafy frail. The world is filled with strangers. Memories fade and so do we. We are deep into the Autumn of our existence. Each day we contemplate our own demise. We dispel our fear as we recall Edmund Rostand's words.

(A light breeze causes the leaves to fall)
CYRANO:
The autumn leaves!
ROXANNE
(Lifting her head, and looking down the distant alley):
Soft golden brown, like a Venetian's hair. —See how they fall!
CYRANO:
Ay, see how bravely they fall,
In their last journey downward from the bough,
To rot within the clay; yet, lovely still,
Hiding the horror of the last decay,
With all the wayward grace of careless flight!

In the year 2003, I can stir up a controversy in a bar by the very mention of the words, "Vietnam"; a place where 58,000 Americans died by the end in 1975 and citizens have not yet come to agreement upon how or why the war was started. "Korea". We lost 53,000 there between 1949 and 1953, (one million South Koreans), and even history books often fail to report properly on that event. Smaller wars produce smaller numbers of casualties and even less mention but they always leave scars upon the families of our own war dead and the dead of the countries in which we fought. They scar our nation. Today, in Iraq, we proceed. Our leaders count the bodies of our enemies as they sort out our friends from our foes. And then there is the count of our own men and women, wounded, dead and emotionally broken. The implications of these wars are never fully known and the human cost in blood and souls defies the most efficient calculation. Have we gained peace or lighted yet another fuse?

***

Men who achieve stations of great authority either nurture or abuse that power. Only after they have exercised that command and, perhaps, passed into history books, can they be called either dictator or liberator; national hero or barbaric despot. Much depends upon who writes the history books.

***

I am in a blues bar in Chicago; a new adventure. With each drink the music seems sweeter; that's fine. Why do such sad lyrics play so well with happy rhythms and smooth chord changes? Why does this depressant taste at once so sweet and yet bitter? Why does the pause between each number seem so long? Why do I want simply to hold the hand of the beautiful woman beside me. Why do I seem to empathize with a form of music I have rarely heard? Why do I want this night to be endless? I do not understand the blues.

***

A man may be "overdressed" or carelessly clothed. He is imperfect. Yet I do not fully trust the man who is exacting in his submission to the fashion of the day. He is a man ruiled by properties, eager to be seen as "correct" and of dubious substance. The finest men care nothing for fashion; in dress or in thought.

***

I never cared where she went or how late she came home or what she had been doing till early morning. The thing was that she came home. She was always kind to me and yielding. She swam in the pool and dozed beneath the blue umbrella and sipped icy, pink wine. She was as beautiful to watch as a cheetah and as native to me as are my eyes or brain. She was not mine anymore than the moon is mine or the ocean to the east of my home. She was with me only to the extent that the meandering sea breeze is with me. I was satisfied with her wandering nature: I had to be. That last night she wanted to swim in the ocean instead of the safe, warm, lighted pool. As usual I acceded to her will. I still can see her white swim suit and her black hair trailing to her waist. I can see her run the last few steps and rush onto the white spray. I see the smooth strokes as she thrust herself into the waves. She disappeared into the darkness. I waited for her till dawn. I never saw her again.

***

I drove by that old house the other day. Remember? The great gray mansion on West Street? The one with the twin turrets? I had not been near there for twenty years or more. The neighborhood is cleaner and more welcoming than it was when we first saw it. Remember that we lied and said we were interested in buying when we called the realtor. She gave us the tour of the empty place and left us there as she hurried to another appointment. We promised to turn the lock on our way out. We tried to make love in the west turret and laughed so much we forgot about love and just lay there and giggled.

Now we could afford the place. It is all fixed up and for sale again. But you are gone and I am alone. One man in a big home like that is a waste of everything. Sometimes I miss you so badly that I want to call. But the anger will not abate; yours nor mine. I hope a happy couple will move in there and have many children to make the rafters squeal with laughter. An old house like that needs love and laughter or it dies. So do people, I think.

***

The theory of evolution states, among other things, that it takes a long time for things and animals and people to evolve. The process is gradual. This is good. And, while I cannot speak for birds, flowers, whales, crickets or frogs, I can say with certainty that a swifter evolution of man would have been resisted to the death. I, for one, like things just as they are!

***

Madrid has a pull on me. I became another person there: more complete. I believe that any new city in any country would have done the same. It is the novelty of the experience that renews the spirit and reveals to us amazing aspects of our nature we had not known before. I like the music and the food, the customs and the ale. I will travel more.

***

It is mid April. Worthless teen-agers drive by with their windows down and play music over their sound systems at a volume so high as to rattle my windows. I remember fifty years ago my doing those things and more and worse. But now is now! Thump, Thump, Thump and not one note! Not one tone. Just Thump! I will get used to it this year as I have for a dozen years. I will begin to worry about the safety of the drivers and their passengers: youngsters with cars. I had better say a quick prayer for them. I hope that God can hear me over the Thump, Thump, Thump..

***

A friend of mine died several years ago. Younger than I, she kept me in touch with the quickly changing world of music and art. She was my link to the new sounds and the latest films and books. She forced me to be contemporary and she taught me tolerance for the new. The many photos I shot of her bedeck the walls of my former studio; now my writing room. I would trash them all tomorrow if I could but hear her voice in my ear and feel her hand in mine.

***

I work in a bullet factory. We are now on overtime. I get paid time and a half for every hour over forty in a week. I can buy another television now.

***

There is a house which, when I see it, seems like a former home to me but which I have never been inside. There was a white convertible I saw in a showroom that I felt I had owned as a young man. I could still hear the purr of the now silent engine and feel the leather seat press firmly against by back. I saw a woman of about twenty years of age dancing in a cabaret several weeks ago whom I thought used to be my lover of forty years ago. When I caught her eye she looked through me as though I were a pane of glass. If I am not insane now, I surely will become so if this trend continues.

***

One of my several character flaws is my intolerance for insults; intended or not. The problem arises when they begin to build up inside me and suddenly I am impelled to unleash my verbal wrath upon him who offended me; perhaps years before. I refrain from confrontations until they virtually explode. This defect of mine has cost me friends. But it has helped me to hang on to my self-respect and retain a good portion of my sanity. I have to work on that deffect.

***

Regarding insults. If they are leveled in public they should be ignored. Let the audience see how rude is the offender. Then the insult should be amended by its target in private so as not to give more embarrassment to the offender. Otherwise, let the offense pass and hope that the fool will continue his loose ways and suffer the just punishment of a person less forgiving than yourself.

***

I have several friends who have physical deficiencies. I do not know if they are drawn to me or I to them. I help them along as best I can and they never fail to add to my sense of usefulness. Such friends are often full of charming wit and an inner joy penned up in broken bodies. They help me as I grope through life, whole in body but lame of spirit. They are good models.

***

Some jazz musicians seem to me to be playing for themselves: self indulgent. These are the ones who go so "far out" that I, with a well trained ear, cannot fly with them. I get lost. Then there are those who play hackneyed riffs and trite "take off's". They seem lazy, unimaginative and never get off the ground. Perhaps I am hard to please. Most of my experiences have convinced me that the best players love to go into uncharted territory with a calm and confident grip and to carry us with them. *Together* we fly beside them, wind in our faces, amazed, looking down on Earth and marveling at what it is that keeps us soaring. We feel safe in their hands. Then they gently bring us home.

***

The law of reciprocation applies to human life as well as mechanics. A man who has been humiliated will soon learn to humiliate. A defeated nation will strive to rise again and conquer. A woman scorned will find a way to emasculate. People do not forget; they reciprocate.

***

Watch the windmill turn the stone that crushes the seeds to make the flour. Watch the wind blow the chaff across the field. It feeds the land and the cycle is complete. So in this world we move from seed through the grinding of life and thence, as husks, blown back into the earth. We live a while as bread, people are fed: we die. Only the wind is indispensable.

***

The Greek goddess Diana is associated with the moon, with virginity and hunting. These first two aspects of her character can be seen in the courtship and wooing of today's young, quivering ladies. Then she is lethal when, in a rage of jealously, she releases from her bow one of the magic arrows drawn from her quiver. I think I was married to her once.

***

You may flee East into tonight or West into tomorrow. Go North or South, into jungles or sandy beaches or snow-topped mountains or verdant valleys. Go where you wish but do not think you are running away. You are merely carrying yourself and your plight with you to be transplanted into new ground. Stay home. Save your money and solve your problems.

***

Wretched is the man whose associates or employees reflect a class of people whom he would not welcome into his home.

***

About one hundred years ago the automobile did not exist. (I looked up the word "car" in a dictionary dated 1895 and there it showed only a railroad car!) Then fuel, tires, steel for roads, bridges, tunnels, motels, trailer parks, city sprawl and more and more roads and … you know the rest. Then wars for oil and steel and rubber and let's build a road around the world and from Juneau, Alaska to Tierra del Fuego. We are slaves to our cars and we scamper to the cotton fields to earn our keep; to pay for our mobile masters.

***

When a woman is born she has within her every egg she will ever produce. Therefore her eggs begin to age immediately. She does, indeed, live her reproductive life on a "time clock". A man may generate new, fresh sperm on into his eighties; billions of them! Each spermatozoa is capable of fertilizing an egg of a female. A man can fertilize (let's say) an egg a day. A woman can produce (let's say) a baby a year. Let's stop fighting about the equality of the sexes. Surely they are equal in rights and privileges, equal in the eyes of God and the law, equal in their value to the species, but they are as different as midnight and noon: both required to make a day. They are both required (so far as I know) to make a baby. Both together are preferred optimally to raise a family. This is why there is romantic love and the joy and sorrow of it. Men and women will always be different. It is their essential difference that defines them. It is their instinct to reproduce that joins them and provides the basis for their desire to remain united forever.

***

Lawyers have so infested the general populace that they gather now in legislatures to pass more laws that will require their further, costly intrusion into our lives. It is to them a matter of preservation of their species. They breed like blow flies and have the same, acute sense of smell.

***

You might well trust a man with your accounts whom you would not trust with your wife, and vice versa. It depends upon the man, the accounts and the wife.

***

Nothing can bring the look of recititude to the countenance of a "proper" woman more quickly that an encounter with a "loose" woman. So stern is her appraisal that one wonders if it be moral reproach or simple envy that inspires it.

***

There is a challenge in acting the classics: to make the hero and his world accessible to a contemporary audience. The opposite problem also exists: to portray a contemporary man and carve that character into a classic figure. A few actors have accomplished both.

***

We have no control over our parentage. We are lucky or unlucky. Sooner or later we must become our own parent. From then on we are responsible and can never again blame or credit "Fate".

***

Life has taught me to trust no one. Least of all, myself.

***

Very few scientific events may truly be called "discoveries". Science and its practicioners progress by building upon the foundations laid by others. All innovation is but a dot along a continuum; merely an advancement.

***

I see that female actors now wish to be called "actors" rather than "actresses". They used to be called "waitresses" and "aviatrixes" and "stewardesses". They got that changed. Now they want to be known as "actors", except at the annual Academy Awards prizes where they still receive "Best Actress" awards. separate from male "actors". If they were consistent they would be "Actors" in that venue, competing with Robert DeNiro and Jack Nicholson, Anthony Hopkins, etc. Women do seem to have a special way of reasoning to go along with their special way of getting their way.

***

I have loved someone whom I knew I could never hold, nor even be with for any certain time. She was beyond my reach and she exceeded my grasp. Yet I love her still. She is gone. Her absence stimulates, clarifies, purifies, and solidifies my love for her. She is perfect in my memory and my love remains undiminished *because* she is absent. My love remains pure and uncorrupted. I will always love her. I am lucky ever to have met her.

***

There are certain people with whom we must converse from time to time. Not only are these conversations dull and unproductive but afterward, when we are alone, we feel somehow diminished by having exchanged pleasantries with them. I learn more by talking to myself than by chatting with these folks and I get less argument.

***

"THESE BRAVE MEN SACRIFICED THEIR LIVES TO PROTECT THE COUNTRY THEY LOVED"

These were not men but mostly boys. They did not sacrifice their lives; their lives were ripped from them, blown out of them and stolen from them under false pretenses. Brave they were but terrified as their flesh was torn apart. They were not protecting their country, as they might have thought; not even protecting the idea of their country. They were protecting the *interests* of their country. Such interests they never fully understood. They were brave boys bamboozled by old, crafty politicians who, by tomorrow, will have forgotten the names of the dead as they busily concoct another charade. And the enemy? Mostly young boys more afraid of their superiors than of death. God bless the dead boys and girls and shame on all the leaders.

***

The value of material wealth is taught us in our youth. It is acquired from post adolescence into middle age, husbanded into old age and allotted to our heirs upon our death. Wealth is like longevity in that they are both much valued by so many. But in the end both are gone. Did we forget to live?

***

By my calendar we are a month into spring. Up here we climb out of winter slowly. The sun performs as expected; it moves north on time and peeks through a certain skylight at my kitchen table at about noon today. But winter does not die without a fight. Today the wind is from the northeast, gusty and chilled. It will abate in a day or so but for now it is a reminder of things to come. This Spring I will stack wood, patch the chimney, seal up windows and buy a new quilt from Mrs. Wilkins. Summer will come and I will be lazy for a while but I must prepare for yet another winter. Today's winds are welcome. Winter sends them to me as a reminder that her journey south is only temporary.

***

My mother and father died within a year of each other at age eighty-five. That was over a decade ago. They were decent, high-minded, upstanding people and I still obey them in matters of thrift, moderation and respect for my elders. I am a much better student now than I was in school. They would be proud of these things in me. But I have also violated their teachings in ways that shame me. I pray that they are unaware of how I have failed them.

***

The most perfect mate for me may live on the other side of the world or just across the road. How am I to know? There is most probably no perfect mate for any of us. It is by working toward perfection in ourselves that we are worthy of the mate who has chosen us. We are lucky to have found a lifelong companion. It will take dedication to that person and to the marriage itself for the union to survive. Each day we will then approach more closely the ideal, knowing that perfection is not to be found on Earth.

***

A friend tells me that when you multiply:
111,111,111 by 111,111,111
you get:
12,345,678,987,654,321.

***

Music has effects upon us which are indescribable. We try but words fail us. The way to describe music is to play and listen to music. My moods are quieter now than were those of my youth but I still hear the youngsters blast away with their music players and I remember. I hate the sounds but I do remember my mother, struggling to be heard above the din emanating from my room: "Please turn that down! It sounds like there is a war going on!" Excuse me. I have to tell the neighbor kids to turn down the volume. I think there is a war...

***

I am plagued by old grudges: offenses given me months or even years ago. My problem is whether to forget them (repress them), forgive them (I cannot seem to do that) or act upon them by calling them to the attention of those who have given me insult. I have indeed confronted an offender or two and later regretted my peevishness. When I hold the anger inside, I feel both violated and impotent. Either way I seem to lose. God, if I cannot forgive, at least grant me the power to forget.

***

The first step toward knowledge of any subject, and for some the most difficult, is to admit ignorance.

***

In life you will acquire only those things which you feel you deserve and will never retain boons of which you feel undeserving. Man's innate sense of justice points the way. Self-esteem is inestimable. To achieve it, we each must deserve it and *know* that we deserve it.

***

The truest test of tolerance is to listen with attention and patience to a monologue espousing a position with which you totally disagree.

***

If you are lost in the city, finding your way back home can be a frightening yet exciting adventure. When you are lost in love, you are frightened and excited but always happy as long as you lover is beside you. Your lover is both your compass and your final objective.

***

I can trust a carpenter who has lost, in part or in whole, one finger in the plying of his trade. He will be both thoughtful and careful. Yet I shun the wood-worker who has two or more damaged digits. He is careless and a slow learner.

I have had pet dogs and/or cats ever since I was born and until I was about fifty-five years old. Over the years perhaps, two dozen (including litters of young). Then I gave them up. Within several years my family lost a Border Collie who was shot by a farmer who thought Buddy was killing sheep, I took our old Scottie, a pal for years, to be euthanaised when he could no longer function and we lost my son's young Golden Retriever to heart worms. Lastly, my Siamese cat died of a stomach cancer. I have owned no pets since. You adopt them, you raise them, you love them and then you lose them. The companionship is not worth the heartbreak. I live alone now. I feed birds and squirrels from feeders and the chipmunks scour for scraps. The deer and raccoons I feed in my back yard are not my pets; the mothers and youngsters simply visit nightly. I feed them corn and raisins but I will not name them.

***

In art, a woman is most attractive when depicted at rest; a man when in action. In life, a woman draws our attention and presents herself as desirable when in action but now it is the pensive, dreaming, restful man who is still and most pleased.

***

"The absolute yearning of one human body for another particular body and its indifference to substitutes is one of life's major mysteries." — *Iris Murdoch*

Ms. Murdoch has pinpointed the anomaly which is at the core of the "Love at first sight" experience. Some people never encounter it. Others do and still others fall under its spell more than once. I admit to belonging to the last group. Excessive, uncontrolled imagination is most probably the culprit where I am concerned. Sparing the reader the details, I can state that I am still in love (with reduced intensity), with four of these women but rarely see them. In my memory it was the blast of love (or covetous) that, like a hot, sweet, narcotic wind seemed nearly to render me first immobile then simply weak and unable to stop staring, (open-mouthed, no doubt), at what seemed a vision of Beauty nearby. I would have gladly died just to please them. One more thing: it is a "thing". I had the experience once more; in my fifty-seventh year. I saw a house that I knew I must own. Months later, fortune worked her miracle and I moved in. I am in my twelfth year of residence here and I hope to stay till I die. I am at last monogamous; loyal to my one home.

***

One who inherits wealth is fortunate but by no means yet secure. Security will come only when he knows how to use money for his own development as a man and for the betterment of mankind. He need not spend it or give it away; he must merely invest it in such a manner as to be useful to others in their lives. Such a man has been blessed. For equipoise he must learn to bless others. Wise men know this. They taught me.

***

In our service to God we often transgress and seek absolution. So our children err and seek (and always receive), our complete forgiveness. Through repetition of the cycle of error and absolution there comes ever-growing trust and loyalty between us. We are then able to guide them down the path further on. We can become coequals with our offspring so that we may stride through life together. Perhaps they will guide us when our own step becomes unsteady.

***

Old men make wars. Young warriors die and innocent civilians perish along with their children and grandparents. Blood runs in the streets and into the mud of the forests and the deserts. In the process one nation assumes dominance over another and there is no victory. The blood of all the victims nourishes the hatred that will bid the next generation to cry out for more blood. War is as certain and as awful as any natural disaster, yet it is only for the catastrophe of war that wise, old men must accept full responsibility.

***

Why are we surprised when arrogance and stupidity reside together in the same brain? They are both required for a leader to imagine that he can change his country or the world for the better by repressing those who do not agree with him. Stupidity is required for arrogance to flourish and arrogance leads men foolishly to reach for the unattainable. History is replete with the stories of men who have overreached their power and became the victims of their own ego. At the core of these men is stupidity. Be careful, America.

***

Do not be ashamed to wish. The wish is often prelude to the act which can culminate in the fact. Move then from the wish to the action and on to the attainment. Look about you! All man-made things began with a wish!

***

If you want to hear a lengthy monologue, ask a man what he thinks or ask a woman how she feels.

As a dictionary holds within it every word you will ever need to say whatever needs to be said, so the piano hides within it every song you will ever sing and all the music you will ever dream. Save time in your day to play your piano.

***

The fact that we can kill a fly with one swat does not make us better than the fly; it only proves that we are stronger and, perhaps, smarter. So one nation may be stronger and wiser in the ways of battle. Does this mean that it is justified in waging war against more primitive peoples? Perhaps so. Perhaps not. But when the neighborhood bully becomes the enemy of all, he then may be justly destroyed by the allied weak? Perhaps. And when he is dead, may not the jackal and his carrion kinfolk gain a feast?

***

When viewing the relationship between the sexes, always remember the architectural slogan: The basic rule of any design is: "Form follows function." So we love each other's form and profit in each other's function.

***

In the practice of medicine, *triage* is the process by which the most urgent yet most successfully treated illness or diseases are attacked first due to the always limited resources of manpower and money. Those with only minor injuries are set aside for later attention. The hopeless are afforded little attention; mere comfort. If a disease is ninety percent fatal and no cure is known, and if that disease affects only two percent of the populace, then the money and energy are diverted to the many cases which are easily curable. In this way, more are cured. Hopeless patients are left in the merciful hands of God. May He have mercy on them and take them straight to Heaven.

***

It is a fact that certain "small" movies have an impact disproportionate to their cost and initial distribution. Conventional wisdom says that the more money you spend, the better the product. Not so in films. Often a director is given full reign over low budget movies and he is able to project his own, unadulterated vision upon the finished product. We are able to look directly into the mind of one man and see clearly his dream and we connect in a very personal manner. Our relationship to the film becomes intimate.

***

If you want to learn about the youth of your now middle-aged friend, observe how he watches the clock and frets over the momentary lateness of his daughter's return from an evening out with her young man.

***

Great actors are alike in this: They are able to create a character who conforms completely to the director's vision of what that character should be and how that character fits, as a puzzle piece, into the overall work. Be they leading actor or character actor, they are as important to the play as one wheel is to an automobile. A great play is peopled by great actors who know their place and fill it well; fit it perfectly.

> "The fourth spear carrier from the left should believe that the play is all about the fourth spear carrier from the left."
> Sir Laurence Olivier.

***

When preparing for a crucial diplomatic encounter, avoid talking about what you are going to talk about.

***

The Bible speaks of the sins of Man. Is Man the only animal capable of sin? Of the millions of species which have come and gone from this planet is it only man who can affront God? Is it only man who is threatened with damnation? It seems that being human, along with its gift of "dominion over the animals" is cursed by the threat of eternal damnation for his tendency to err.

***

My renunciation of women has come too late. I have five children from three wives and I owe everyone money. I am old and tired and of no use now. I sleep mostly. I am through with women!

***

Over the many centuries man has invented a god for that which he could not comprehend. A sun god, a moon goddess, a rain god, a fire god, a god of the harvest, a god of love, a river god, a volcano goddess and many others. Then, as man slowly began to understand and even predict these events, the gods gradually were eclipsed by knowledge. Now God has been left with the truly important, imponderable questions of the "Why?", the "How?"and the "When?" We will need God for quite a while now. Perhaps forever. Does God need us?

***

"Second childhood" is often attributed to the failing of the mind; a sort of brain atrophy revealed in early stages by bold, often unrealistic desires and a forgetfulness of the day or hour, yet with clear memories of days long past. "Dotage", some call it or "senility". As I approach this period of life I rather think that I will be remembering the things that were and are very important to me: my mother's songs, my father's hands, a meadow and a ball I caught to the cheers of the crowd. I will recall a certain poem word for word. I will remember the girl who sat in front of me in the second grade who let me fondle her braids. I will recall all the important things.

***

At about twelve days, the embryo of a pig, a chicken, a fish and a human appear about the same to the untrained eye. Each lies in a saline solution. Slowly, each begins to become more easily distinguishable. At about three months the chimpanzee and the human embryo still look almost alike. At birth it is man who will be dominant on the planet. Yet avoid arrogance. In another time you might have been born a Rhode Island Red rooster. Do not waste this miracle. Become as human as you can as soon as you can, remembering always that there is an animal flourishing within you.

***

To study one's own history is to turn over every stone and be prepared to view such awful as may be found there. Any honest autobiography will contain some shocking material. Man is imperfect by his very nature. All great heroes exhibit great faults. Only the dead are perfect.

***

Contact your friends more often. Imagine standing by a grave thinking, "I should have stayed in touch more often. I forgot to tell him I loved him."

***

Atheism is a sign of man's ultimate rebellion against his father.

***

The urge to possess the object of one's passion is never tempered by wisdom. Yet one person cannot possess another. The mind knows this but the body insists. So, when passion abates, we are left owning only our memories. If we are lucky, we are in the company of a friend who loves us and whom we love.

***

Dreams are the subconscious unleashed. Wild, magical, frightening and beautiful things happen to us in our dreams. When morning comes, sometimes we remember but often we forget our wondrous visions. Our subconscious has been chatting with us. I wish I could remember all my dreams.

***

If a man has been annoying you, pestering you with his petty problems and generally making a nuisance of himself, loan him as much money as you can afford to lose. With any luck at all, you will never see him again.

***

Promise her anything. Then prepare to keep those promises and always regret having made them. Or break those promises and regret that breach forever. Either way you are in for great pain. Simplify. Promise her nothing and require no promise in return.

***

I stand on the beach in Key Biscayne. I look eastward toward Nassau, far beyond the horizon. I am a fair swimmer. I want to swim to the Bahamas for a drink. It's about eighty miles, I guess. The current and the sharks and barracuda will present problems, of course. I can just strip down, wade out and stroke my way to the next landfall. My wife calls me to dinner. I turn from the blue sea and walk up the path to our home. Perhaps tomorrow.

***

If you wish to be free, associate with those who crave independence. Select a woman who has a passion for liberty. Leave the door ajar and throw open the windows. She will stay with you for as long as she feels free to leave.

***

When you are young, with a family, there is not enough money: ever. You strive and she works at home and away from home. Somehow the children grow up, get their education and get married. They are on their own. Yet you have developed the habit of making money. There is not enough money to do the things deferred till now. Money for retirement and that trip abroad. You earn a good income but that is not enough. You have acquired the habit of focusing on money, developed when you were impoverished, and practiced now out of inclination. You are addicted to money. Can you kick that habit? It will be difficult but worth the effort. We all die broke.

***

By the manners, the grammar and the cleanliness of the children you may know much about the parents.

***

DROPS OF WATER, GRAINS OF SAND

Nature takes care of itself if left alone. My family needs attentive nurturing. Sometimes I get the two conditions confused. My wife reminds me.

***

Borrowing money is a serious matter. Your first loan is the first line in your credit report. From this point on you will be known as either credit worthy or a bum. There is no in-between. Nurture your credit worthiness.

***

Let the people who love Nature protect it most by leaving it alone.

***

A pileated woodpecker is at my seed feeder. These birds eat bugs and mites. What does he do with seeds? He picks out one sunflower seed. He flies to an oak tree about ten feet away and wedges the seed into a small groove of bark. He then pecks open the shell to get at the meat. His sharp bill and the wedge, together in the tree, yield welcome variety to his diet. The tree is his work bench. His beak; his hatchet. His scarlet cap covers a fine brain.

***

The war is over. The losers founder in a broken world with no means for rebuilding their country. All the spent money and lives on both sides are assigned to the past. The victors dig into their coffers again to help rehabilitate the vanquished as both nations attempt to achieve the "status qou ante."

***

Motion pictures combine images and sound. They are capable of entertaining, teaching and exciting. They are able to evoke emotions and dreams. They can carry us far away or send us on an adventure into our own mind. Movies are magic mirrors into which we may peer to find ourselves.

***

In the village the elders convene to plan out the new well, the crops to be planted, the huts to be rebuilt and the orphans to be relocated within the village family. There is no time for tears. Daily prayers are dutifully chanted but belief has been tested to its limits. There is not one person in this village who can say why this last war was begun nor how it stopped nor who won.

***

In war as in criminology one should "follow the money". When all is tallied up, where did the money go? There is a body count and new border lines assigned, there are war crimes trials and lists of the missing. There are numbers to account for the civilians dead and injured, but where is the money? Who accumulated all the money that was spent?

In Winter I watch a certain tree in my backyard. It is dwarfed and more than a bit crooked. Its twisted limbs lie naked to the wind and covered with ice and snow. It looks like it may not live. Yet in Spring the green buds appear and then leaves. It stretches its arms up toward heaven and seems to be thanking Someone for the gift of yet another year. I am pleased.

***

Let those who earn their wealth by stripping the planet be called by the name that suits them best: "Thief". Their children will live to call them so.

***

Motives and means may be in logical dispute. Aesthetics and ethics are surely debatable but a fact is not subject to interpretation or argument.

***

There is, indeed, "true love" between man and woman. It is rare but so is gold. Therefore, when it is realized, guard it as you would the golden band it represents. Nurture it as you would a rare orchid. Place nothing above it. Someday it will be attenuated by death but till then... love.

***

There have been wars throughout history. As man "progresses", the wars become more lethal and body counts more significant. Some say there will always be wars. This will be true till enough people cry, "Enough!"

***

Free Will or Determinism. We feel that we act from freedom of the will but we know full well the power of causality. We kiss them because we want to. We kiss them because they tell us in their secret way that they want to be kissed. It is part of the mating ritual designed many millions of years ago. We are driven by our past but each step into the future seems voluntary. This problem has never occupied my mind as it might have.

***

Be generous with the man who carries away the trash, the boy who mends your roof and the nurse who tends you when you are ill. They perform tasks you will not or cannot do. They enable you to better perform your profitable duties. Thank them and pay them well.

***

The array of musical instruments has been developed over the centuries in order to speak to the many moods of our mind. We have so much to say and so many ways to speak that we require not just our own voices but the magical instruments of music. If music speaks directly to the soul, then instruments must be devised which can express the messages. Recall the concert orchestra of one hundred instruments speaking to the spirit of the audience. Remember the piano solo in the late night cocktail lounge. Words just won't do.

***

I tried a certain taboo drug one night. It was exciting. The whole evening became a series of wonderful dream-like events. The dinner was the best ever; the wine tart yet tender. The women; the most beautiful. The music came to my ears directly from God. My new companions became friends for life. Our conversation was filled with witticisms and epigrams; in need of a stenographer. It was full morning before the bliss subsided. I shall never forget that night and I will never take that drug again.

***

Two wives: fine women of great beauty and charm. Good mothers they were. They discovered before I did that I was not fit to be a mate or a father. Now I live alone. Now they and I and guilt are strangers.

***

My circle of friends is diminishing. I lose out to death, geography, indifference and my own selfish interests. I am turning inward because I need time alone to be who I want to be and do what I want to do. I give no time away but husband it for myself. I miss my friends and remember them with fondness but I luxuriate within my solitude. I am ashamed I am so selfish.

***

Among the best of friends there exists a mutually held streak of competition. Among the most fierce of enemies there is often respect for each other's courage, audacity and boldness. All around the ironies abound.

***

When one child goes hungry, shame is justly heaped upon the community.

***

The termination of a love affair,
Be it painful or otherwise,
Is like the late March frosty air.
It is another beginning in disguise.

***

Military Brats. One or more of their parents is in the service and is regularly transferred from one military base to another. The children are uprooted and dragged along. The youngsters hardly have time to make friends with anyone but their parents. Like an anchor, they ride with the ship to whatever destination, wherever destiny sends them. They are dropped into strange waters and expected to rest there till hauled up again. They also serve.

***

Some men smell out the source of power and, like salmon in autumn, follow the aroma upstream into the halls of authority. Others seek out the weak and impoverished and struggle to aid the hungry and the oppressed. Should the mighty ever become compassionate, or the gentle become powerful, we would see a new Golden Age. To wish that is not a bad thing.

***

The novels and stories of John Steinbeck are so vivid in their moods, settings and dialogue that they needed almost no rewriting to become scripts for films. He wrote for the eye and the ear and the heart. "Of Mice and Men" has been filmed three times, "East of Eden" twice, "The Grapes of Wrath", "The Red Pony", "The Moon Is Down" and "The Pearl" made one time each and several short stories were combined to make movies; i.e., *Tortilla Flat* and *Cannery Row*. He wrote the original screenplay for *Viva Zapata* (1952) with an understanding of revolution and its aftermath that we would see played out again and again in life, just as it had been in his biographical screenplay. We are lucky to have had him to write about us.

***

Make a vow to yourself and honor it. God will esteem you. But if you should break a covenant with yourself, how is God ever to trust you?

***

You read books and newspapers and poetry as a child. Instruct your children to do likewise. And when the children are grown and gone, take time to write. Write short letters, family histories, words of encouragement to the children and love notes to your spouse. Reading and writing are mated.

***

Take care of your physical and emotional needs. If you should fail to fulfill these needs, how then can you be expected to care for your mate and the children who count on you? If the hunter cannot hunt, who will feed the family?

*** *

I was married to a loving wife. The children from that union were grown and gone away. I met a young lady. We fell in love. My marriage was dissolved and I quickly wedded my new love. I should have stayed married to my first wife and had an illicit affair with the younger woman. The Bible says "No", but common sense and a loud voice in my head cries, "Fool!"

***

When you lose everything you love, you love even more everything you have lost. So carelessness breeds caring and heartlessness breaks a heart. Everything happens for the best, I suppose, but it always seems too late.

***

The birth of a nation is not a pleasant thing to describe. Its enthusiastic conception was filled with joy, promise and hope. Details of its ensuing delivery can be a bit too distasteful for polite conversation.

***

Hamlet's soliloquy lives on for four centuries. The problem is universal. Whether to face Life as it comes rushing at you or to leap into Death as an escape. The logic of Hamlet's thinking is flawless but his conclusions on the matter are not so clear; nor is the play. Ophelia's demise is set forth as an enigmatic event. Hamlet's own death is seen as a tragedy. Too much dying all around. I will stick to Shakespeare's comedies.

***

On the subject of dreams; there are some that are so exciting and beautiful that I fear to wake but finally do. Then there are those which terrify or sadden me so deeply that I struggle to awaken but cannot. These dreams are trying to tell me something. Why are my dreams different from yours? They are messages to me from my subconscious and, to the extent that I remember them and think them through, they are secrets revealed and not to be ignored. Before clocks and deadlines we had time to reflect upon our dreams. Steal back the time.

***

I still can hear my mother and my father as they told me stories of their own childhoods. Almost all the stories they told were amusing and made me laugh. Some were sadder. Life was so very different two generations ago. Things change so rapidly now that I fear the old stories will neither entertain nor instruct the children of today. If this is true, I feel sorry for them.

***

The tragedy of democracy is that only those who feel superior to their fellow man have the strength and the will to become elected leaders. Such dedication to superiority ill befits "a nation of laws, not of men." Arrogant men, disguised as public servants, rule all nations.

***

An actor will never admit to the public that he "steals" a bit from other actors but each knows that his on-stage performances are sprinkled with affectations he has seen in his studies. It is the way these are selected and combined with his own inventive skills that results in his totally believable performance. In every career we all build on the knowledge of others.

***

In all undertakings we seek personal fulfillment. It is the successes, I suppose, for which the efforts are long remembered. However, if we examine our memory we will recall that it was at the moment when we *decided* to go forth upon our mission that was the most exciting. Committing to the success of our journey was the flash of brilliant light. We saw clearly each obstacle as a stepping stone toward our goal. It was at this moment that we felt most invigorated and powerful. Our hearts pounded. We were afraid but brave. Win or lose; it is that moment of commitment that we remember.

***

Life is comprised of time. I waste it as though it were inexhaustible. Some parse it out on schedule cards: eat at 6:00 a.m., leave for the office at 6:45 AM, arrive at office by 8:00 AM, coffee break at 10:00 AM, etc. Home at 6:45 PM. Supper at 7:30 PM, read newspaper and to bed at 10.00 PM sharp. I do not know which way is right. I seem to get enough done in one day to satisfy my needs. An appointment is a yoke around my neck and an alarm clock is my sworn enemy. I expect to live by whim till I am eighty. If I die sooner I will then be in no state to regret my prodigality.

***

He who trusts no one is most likely not to be trusted.

***

Some of the most professional actors slip now and then and actually fall in love with their on-stage female partners. I attribute this failing to their complete involvement with their roles. It is very unprofessional but, like a policeman turned vigilante, they simply get too involved in their work. Among them: Bogart, Brando, Burton, Grant, McDowell, McQueen, Newman, Olivier, Sellers, Tracy and a lot more.

***

Procrastination in the adolescent is an unforgivable vice. Prepare, act, learn, do the proper thing now. This should be the credo of the young man or woman. Then in the middle years, events drive the actions. Obligations to the children, the parents, the friends and business associates must and will be met in a timely manner. For the old folks things will be different. Watch the sunset, walk the beach, fish the lake, write the poem, linger outside the old, family home. Take the time to phone old friends and take the time to listen to them brag about their grandchildren. Loaf your life away if you wish. Or bustle about your world tying up loose ends, making new friends. Do as you please, but spare yourself the tyranny of the time clock. Put off some distasteful tasks until tomorrow. Soon there will be no tomorrow and all chores can be justly left behind. Others will see to them. Welcome the ultimate procrastination.

***

Some individuals have learned, perhaps from youthful experiences, that hiding from reality is the best option. They search about for a safe place where memories may be repressed and reality can be shaped to conform to their liking. They crave order in a world which they find to be chaotic. They search for serenity within the madhouse of the marketplace. They crave the sublime. If fortunate, they become our authors, artists, actors or musicians.

***

I know too much. That's not good. I've been just about everywhere I want to go. No sense going back to see how things have changed. One look in a mirror will show me that. The love I want no longer exists for me. My desires are "unrealistic" and my needs are so well provided that I lack that spark which used to roll me out of bed in the morning to battle the dragons of the workplace. Somehow, between now and death I must find a way to pass the time. Perhaps I will buy a dog. I will not name him.

***

I saw her for no more than a minute or two. She was ahead of me in line, checking into my hotel. I mean our hotel. Dark red hair, white suit, long legs, exquisite hands. Then she turned: blue eyes, dark eyebrows, wide mouth, dark lipstick. She was shaped like an athlete; a swimmer. She smiled as we almost touched; gleaming, white teeth. She strode toward the cocktail lounge, a bit early for a drink. I began to check in and momentarily forgot my name. The clerk smiled as if he knew something I did not. I had my baggage sent up to my room and stepped toward the bar. I paused. A bit early for a drink. I retreated.

***

I am ambivalent about women. What sane man is not? Ergo: Only insane men fall in love. And I think all women are inscrutable to men because their wants and needs are so different from our own. I knew a woman once, she said, "You are the kind of man I would have liked to have had an affair with but would never have married." How about that! And they say women are more romantic than men! I was married. Was it romance? Security? Intellectual stimulation? My ability to provide financially for her and our children? Was it these that drew her to me? Well, I failed in all categories. I am single now and I am looking for a woman who would like to have an affair with me but would not want to marry me. So far, no luck.

***

All women want to marry. All women who want children want to marry. All women without a good job want to marry. All women without a steady job want to marry. All women whose friends are all married want to marry. All women whose mothers nag at them to get married may want to get married but will not, in order to spite their mothers. This last group is my favorite.

***

I have more books than I will ever read, more recorded music than I will ever hear and more movies than I will ever watch. As sure as I give some of these things away I will want them back. So I hang on to things which occupy space and I feel miserly. I will find a way to escape this trap or die in the trying.

***

A second marriage for a widower pays honor to his first wife. A second marriage to a divorced man is suspect and borders on panic. A third; suicidal and ought to be illegal

***

By writing, I close the door to my friends. Then I begin to wonder, "Where have all my friends gone?" Now is the time for me to be alone and hold a mirror to my life and select thoughts that are of importance to me and write them down. If others find my thoughts worth their time, that will be fine.

***

As a young college student I paid more attention to the beautiful girls than I did to my studies. My test scores and grades attest to that fact. I did, however, save every textbook I ever owned. Now that pretty girls are of no carnal interest to me (nor I to them), I am reading again those dusty textbooks and I find that they are quite instructive. If I had read them back then, my life might have been very different. Who is there who would never turn back a clock?

A movie-maker puts all his effort into the production of a work. He puts his personal mark on the film and his name on the credits. After a few weeks in theaters it is sold to television, hacked into bits by commercials and finally forgotten. It must be devastating to witness the slaughter of your child accompanied by the sound of loose change jingling in your pocket.

****

All card games have rules. Most have prescribed etiquette. These two components imply a sort of politeness. In card games played by serious players, rules and etiquette are assiduously observed while, beneath the civility, the annihilation of all opponents is the common objective.

****

A man may have one home for his whole life. He may move many times, from home to home. He may have a mobile home which he can carry with him as he moves from place to place. Our only true home is inside us. If we have built it soundly and maintained it well we will always be welcome there.

****

In a movie about the military ethos, a high ranking officer is testifying at a Court Martial, and, in a response to a demand by a counsel for the "truth", he barks out, "You can't handle the truth!" (*A Few Good Men*, 1992). Sometimes I wonder if anyone can handle the truth. So novels, spiritualists, tarot cards, crystal balls, etc. Truth has successfully eluded Man since he first appeared on Earth. If he were ever to be confronted with the Absolute Truth he would not know how to respond. He simply could not handle the truth.

****

Learning to read at an early age is crucial. More desirable is loving to read. A passion for reading will cost little and instruct much. It can produce innumerable benefits for those of any age. This cannot be said of most passions.

****

I sold a stock at a bit more than I had paid for it. Then I watched as it went up in price. Up and up. Each day I watched and mourned, not my loss (which was nonexistent), but my failure to gain. I then remembered advice given to me long ago. "When you sell a stock at a profit be happy. Do not watch the stock after you have sold it. Let the next fellow make some money too."

When a stalwart friend dies, I die a bit too. He takes with him the laughter of our shared foolery. My sounding board is gone. One less pal to worry about me.

***

I pictured a curving walkway. A snaking, red-brown, brick trail to take me down gently; down from my home to the riverside. Pinpoint lights to guide me in the nights. There would be a bench for two. The idea became an apparition and I could see it clearly in its aesthetic perfection; all rustic and trimmed by deep green myrtle, with the oaks clasping arms overhead, and I, in the evening strolling down with a cool drink to watch the ducks prepare for darkness. The image was sublime.

Yet I will not build the walkway. I will not transform my private reverie into reality. I will stand by the window and dream the dream. I will nightly envision that perfect path while I imagine that I hold tightly to your small hand. I will fantasize and watch us walk together downward to sit beside the gray water. There will be no need to speak.

***

To write a sonata a man must battle himself. To write an opera man must struggle with the world. To write a symphony man must be at war with God. As the composer struggles, he seeks only to be at peace.

***

The greatest warriors may be found quietly awaiting reinforcements, or busy tending young recruits, or crying over a dying comrade, or giving comfort in a field hospital, or negotiating at the peace table. There is much more to war than killing. All great warriors excel at war and worship peace.

***

A play is written to be played; to be seen and heard. Yet there are plays which are read with much enjoyment and reward. Our minds create the sets, select the costumes and the voices of the characters. Our minds set the pace of the drama and the implied action is only as exciting as we need; the deaths only as brutal as is necessary for us. The love scenes are sufficient to our taste. Plays are published in books. Favorite scenes are there for deeper examination. All the playwrights: Sophocles, Shakespeare, Molier, Miller, O'Neil, Williams, Inge, Ibsen, are there in the library. We can become the designer and director of our own production!

***

The news from the warfront is excellent. This week over one thousand of the enemy were killed and our losses were but ninety-seven dead and 211 wounded or missing. This compares to last week when our losses were a bit higher and theirs somewhat lower. We are winning. How long this war will last is up to the enemy. As soon as he surrenders, the war will be over. Although he shows no sign of quitting now, he is weakening. A certain sign of his collapsing military is that he has begun conscripting women and young boys into his army. Time is on our side.

***

We each are born alone and die alone but we will, along the way, become accustomed to the companionship of others. Remember that such social ties are symbiotic and require much giving for gifts received. To be alone can be lonely indeed, but it requires of one merely a tolerance for loneliness.

***

Having unlimited funds results in unlimited choices. Man, being what he is, can grow tired of the problems involved in choosing. Do not expect your wealthy friends to be happy. They have their problems too. Will I exchange my problems for theirs? I am not sure.

***

It is best to remain ignorant of a conjurer's secret deceptions. Amazement has a value beyond knowledge. Awe is both rare and memorable.

***

A couple once in love may someday learn to hate each other. From hate the only direction open is toward tolerance.

***

The mother who bore me and nursed me and tutored me is, some write, the probable root cause of my mental disquietude. Then why do I miss her so much and hear her laughter even over the sound of the rushing waterfall?

***

A young man marries his mother's likeness; a young woman her father's. This is commonly accepted by psychologists. Any deviation from this pattern is liable to produce astonishing, unintended consequences which can be either painful or marvelous. The impulsive, unregulated marriage of two young people is Nature's exhilarating, high stakes gamble.

***

He asked for her hand in marriage because her eyes were the color of the blue-green sea where they had first met; and as fathomless. She accepted because she felt so secure in his arms as they danced one night. Last week I attended a party celebrating their fiftieth wedding anniversary. Their twelve grandchildren are now fully grown.

***

In the final analysis, marriages arranged by the parents are for the best; for the parents, the family bank accounts and for superficial tranquillity... among the parents. The young couple will work things out.

***

The joys and sorrows of motherhood are unique and forever secret from the father.

***

So called "minor infidelities" in a marriage are like a burr under the saddle of a horse. They are painful irritants. If not removed promptly, they can cause sores which may disable the beast permanently. But if we care about the animal and look to his well-being, we will remove the irritant quickly, allowing time for healing, and then enjoy many bountiful years together.

***

How many great authors were lost to us because they died early or were otherwise deprived of time or were never even taught to read?

***

For a marriage to thrive, both partners must love each other, tolerate each other and be loyal. But of greater importance than these is a mutual devotion to the marriage itself. For a marriage to survive, the couple must value the marriage above all else. They must be devoted to the marriage.

***

People write because they believe they have something to say that will inform, instruct or entertain a potential reader. Some write because they must.

Some write in order to learn:
"If you want to learn about a subject write a book about it." (anon.)

***

The only thing worse than owing money is knowing that when the debt comes due there will be insufficient funds for payment.

***

DROPS OF WATER, GRAINS OF SAND

The little, blue flowers that sprout in the Spring and signal the awakening of the myrtle; these are as dependable as the calendar, the position of the Sun relative to Earth, or the arrival from the South of the robin and the hummingbird. Their blossoms are brief but brash and brave against the storms of April.

***

Tornadoes tear through the Central Plains and sweep into the Eastern hills of our nation. They may rip across the North too. Like rosebuds they arrive in the Spring. Sometimes they follow the Autumnal hurricanes that crash into our eastern shorelines adding terror to torment. They seem then to be bent on destroying destruction. In their paths they leave losses of property and life. They regenerate in many a renewed faith in God.

***

There is a crucial gap between fantasy and reality. It must be maintained or, if not, then strictly controlled. Otherwise, the two become intertwined; confused. Chaos ensues in both thought and action. When the two are commingled, love can become hate and our children can become our enemies. Many crimes are committed when fantasy outstrips reality. When fantasy becomes reality man learns to fly above the clouds and he learns how to destroy the planet in a day. When fantasy and reality intermingle there may emerge either another Christ or another Caligula. Be careful.

***

The subconscious is a strong, mysterious animal. If not well trained, it will, like a leashed tiger, take us where it wants us to go. Only constant awareness can hope to control the pull. Stay alert. Listen to your subconscious but never blindly obey the tug. Sometimes nightmares come true.

***

All the wonderful things we have ever dreamed carry on their backs a price and a danger. In our daydreams we neglect the balance and see only the object of our wishes. In reality we often fail entirely to follow our dreams and so fade into the mob anonymously. As we nightdream, we are in a world of metaphor. These dreams tell us what to fear, what to love, how to attain our goals and where the pitfalls lie. How to interpret correctly these dreams is our ongoing task in life. The implementation of any knowledge gained from these interpretations is the agenda of our lives.

***

Some people need to be driven like a mule. Others need to be drawn like a wagon. Still others drive the mule that tows the wagon on which they ride. And then there is the observer.

She died so long ago that one might think I have, by now, moved on past my mourning, past passion, past love; into the world outside my grief. No. Every morning when I wake she seems to die again and I am ever surprised and freshly grieved. I hold on to tangible "tinctures, stains and relics" like one retains saintly vestiges. Someday I may forget her; perhaps even for an hour, but that day is far ahead, over the misty, lonely, empty horizon.

Banner Headline: "New evidence in L.A. Wife's Murder!" Smaller head-line: "56 Die in Kansas Twisters". Beneath the fold: "Over 2 Million die of Aids in Africa!". There is either something wrong in the newspaper or something wrong with those who read the newspaper.

I have forsaken all personal pets. They devour my time, tax my patience and bind me to my home more than I want. I feed them and then dispose of their waste matter. I groom them then watch as they roll around in the dirt. My cats have regularly attacked me for exercise and recreation. The dogs need to be penned or leashed or kept inside when their nature is to roam. Pet snakes scare the girls. Gerbils awake when I go to bed. Tropical fish need more care than a newborn baby. And all pets eventually die. I would not normally bother you with this but I was just now offered a West High-land Terrier puppy as a gift, (I would name her Bitsy), and I need to talk myself out of accepting her. Can you help me?

Logic should be marked, "Handle With Care!" Logic can lead one into areas where reason has no place. Logic is a tool, as cold as the surgeon's blade. Man is not, by his nature, logical. Logic never caused a painting or a flower, a kiss or a child: or a sweet memory. Apply logic to the causes of wars and you will see how useless logic is. Logic is a mere device for solving intellectual problems. Few daily problems are of an intellectual nature. Enthusiasm, instinct, compromise and experience solve more problems in one's life than can an age of cold logic.

The traffic light turns green. Logic says, "Go." Experience and common sense says, "Look both ways and, if all is clear, then go."

For a good citizen, operating within the written law is not enough. He must move about his daily affairs within the spirit of the law.

Words speak the law. The law may be later repealed. Actions, however, have consequences which may never be revoked. Act with care so as to avoid a lifetime of unrelenting, grim regret.

***

Instructions for Roulette, Keno, Slot Machines & Video Poker:

DO NOT PLAY THESE GAMES!

***

The toys of toddlers and the toys of the aged are the only playthings which give joy without costing more than they are worth. For all the other playthings we pay much too dearly.

***

Lies from leaders may destabilize democracies.

***

Overindulgence in anything causes physical problems of one sort or another. Therefore overindulge in only those things which give you enough pleasure to make it worth the degradation of your body. Hedonism and wisdom are not mutually exclusive.

***

I would happily trade all I have to be young again; to have another round of living. I own property and bonds and a summer home but I can find no one to sit down and bargain with me for eternal life. Where on Earth is The Devil?

***

I have an ex-wife whom I still admire greatly. I dream of her often; romantic dreams. I do not worry that she might read this. She will not be certain to which ex-wife I am referring.

***

When I say that I hate this war, the king retorts that I am saying that I hate the warriors. I love the brave warriors and I hate a foolish war that grinds them into meat or turns them into butchers. I hate the "gardens of stone" that hide their corpses. I hate the funereal bugle! I long to hear the harp.

***

Now, in mid April, the first hummingbird has returned. Even now, as I write, only four feet from my face. Just a bit of sugar water and a bright, red feeder draws him here. So small. So fleet. So secretive. Sweet season to you, my friend! More nectar is ready whenever you are!

**

CDs, DVDs, cable modems, disks, diskettes, LED screens, cell phones, digital cable, digital cameras, digital pocket recorders, satellite photos of deer in the field, and women wearing men's neckties. Kamikaze type Airliners rip into towers and explode, killing thousands. Welcome to the 21st Century. My brain is exhausted and my nation is on high alert!

**

Defeating Iraq was accomplished with relative ease. Weeks. Freeing Iraq and installing a representative government may take decades. I hope someone learns something from this adventure. I learned that oil outranks blood in importance.

**

A Generality: It seems to me that women have a natural gift for motherhood. Men have a natural gift for becoming fathers but, having accomplished that feat, they must then study and learn, over time, the complex role of fatherhood. Be patient with them.

**

There is enough of everything for everybody. The inequality in wealth can be accounted for by the disparity in motivation, ingenuity, wit and the instinct for ownership. For the continued evolution of the species this is arguably a benefit. This also explains why the wealthy endow their offspring. They want to perpetuate themselves through their children. These children may have "neither wit nor wisdom" but neither the parent nor society cares. The treasure passes on down to them. So poverty is the legacy of the poor and wealth is the unearned gift to the unproved. So poor children die for lack of care and the rich are made well and live on to rule. This sad situation is merely another example of instinct overcoming empathy. The survival of the fittest means the survival of the children of the fittest. Darwin is again proven to be correct.

**

A bird the size of a robin has been pilfering the food of my hummingbirds. This thief has a brighter breast than a robin and is more handsome in every feature. Still he has a very narrow beak and can penetrate the defenses designed by those who create hummingbird feeders. So he plunders the liquid meant for my diminutive friends. Always championing the underdog, (but never betting on him), I try to defend the feeder from the giant stranger. How foolish. The mixture I feed is four parts water to one part white sugar. The only thing cheaper than sugar is water. Therefore, I will set up enough feeders for every bird in the county! Then I will have a yard full of fat birds with bad teeth. Nature and I will work through these things.

***

I write at night. At my desk I face the east. When the sun rises I know it is time to get to bed. Sometimes, when I am full of myself and at full sail, with the wind of hubris at my back, I stay a while and face the morning; writing away. The sun in morning throws sharp-edged, crisp shadows on the walls: vertical trees, quivering leaves, (windows need cleaning), and now and then birds in flight. This morning a bird perched upon my window sill and I caught its black shadow as it fell upon an old tapestry hanging just to my right. In the woven work was a deer beneath a sprawling tree and on one branch of this tree today, for less than a minute, stayed the shadow of that visiting bird. I saw a charcoal bird on the tree in the tapestry; wings fluttering for a moment and then it was gone, like all birds go. Can I ever look at that wall hanging again without thinking of the little creature? How many birds have thus perched when the sun and the tapestry were so perfectly in line and no eye was there to witness the phenomenon? How many unseen miracles happen about us all the time and we too busy or too sleepy to notice?

***

Life will be simpler when human beings become extinct. It will certainly become so for all the other creatures. That is if there is any life left any-where on earth.

***

When the popularity of any leader exceeds 75% the nation should beware: so should the leader. Hubris is in the air and Ate waits in the wings. Most failed leaders have enjoyed high approval ratings just prior to failure. Their pride teases them into grievous error, reaching beyond their grasp. These leaders believe the polls and erroneously believe in their omniscience and they forget that the mob and the polls are, by their nature, fickle and often wrong.

***

A man in love cannot write about love anymore than an insane man can write about insanity or a dead man of death. Love renders one witless. Objectivity cannot exist where love thrives. Lovers love. That is all they do well.

***

One of the great pains in life is to be asked for aid from one you love and be unable to comply. Save money and time against that day so that you can respond to the cry for help. It is hell to have to deny relief to one you love.

***

I have seen children take their first steps. To the voices of approval they step one, two, three times and fall to the floor. They do not have far to fall; their little bodies are well cushioned with fat. We applaud and they laugh. Their next attempt is better. They look at the floor now, orientating themselves and they achieve six or eight steps this time. Later their new-found mobility impels them to move about the house touching and feeling, "Brailling their world" from one room to the next. Still, they will stumble if they do not watch the floor for orientation. So they stumble. As an old man I stumble sometimes. That is because I am too busy watching the sky and sniffing the wind and hurrying toward a far off horizon. I am too busy to look at the ground beneath me. Such men as I have strolled off the edge of a cliff while photographing a distant waterfall.

***

Today a pair of Mallard ducks arrived on my back deck; one hundred feet above the water. Another pair of birds, which I cannot identify, is raiding the hummingbird feeder. A fox squirrel shares a dish of food with a chipmunk. An old girlfriend phones me. These are signs and portents I have not yet deciphered. Something is about to happen. I fear.

***

Few things embarrass me more than to remind a debtor that he is behind with a payment. The debts are small and the debtor well able to pay. Why then am I so embarrassed? I am ashamed that I ever granted the loan.

***

No matter how clearly one explains the reasons for his inadequacies or misconduct, he is said by most to be making excuses. Reasons and excuses are almost always misconstrued by those hearing them. It is easier to blame than to understand. It is easier to scold than to empathize.

***

The news is bad again today. Every day the news is either frightening or depressing; or both. Good news is that a missing child was found in Oregon or when a man in Michigan wins several million dollars in the state-sanctioned lottery. Why is bad news the stock in trade of newspapers and broadcasting? Because we buy what we like and we like bad news.

***

In visiting a foreign country, it is as important to learn the customs and mores of that culture as it is to learn the language. One can learn enough language to get along but one cannot correct an inadvertent insult or retrieve breach of local etiquette. When visiting other nations, I first learn to say, in the local language, "Please excuse me", "I'm sorry," and "Forgive me."

***

In states that profess democracy, the voter turnout is highest when the voters feel that their votes are crucial. It drops off when the voters begin to believe that their vote will change nothing about the government. As voter interest declines, democracy is indeed in jeopardy. From then only the politicians and their families rule; funded by the wealthy; courted by the clergy.

***

To care for a dying parent is an ancient and laudable tradition. It is expected by society and accepted by the younger adult as a sacred responsibility. It is an affirmation of generational continuity. We care for those who, in our infancy, cared for us.

To attend to the physical and emotional needs of one's dying child is first an aberration and secondarily a daily reminder of the imponderables that are the companions of our very existence. It is an outrage. To watch helplessly one's child die can slowly kill the capacity for joy in the most noble heart.

***

If we take the emotional and religious component out of procreation, we can rationalize infidelity in both men and women. Maximization of the race, combined with diversification, competition and survival, will indeed strengthen the race. Polygamy is, for biological reasons, the only logical goal of maximum production of individuals. Both monogamy and polygamy are practiced in different societies and each is cherished and pronounced as "good" by those who practice each. Variance of belief is as crucial to the furtherance of existence as is biological diversity. It is those who preach monogamy, yet live a polygamous existence, who are engaging in hypocrisy.

In comedy there are racial and ethnic stereotypes. This has been so since language was spoken and racial and ethnic differences were observed. Furthermore such humor is practiced within an ethnic, religious or racial society by members of that society. It in only when negativity is attached to the joke that it becomes worthy of objection. Those who cannot tell the difference have no sense of propriety and no sense of humor.

***

A bout of heavy drinking can bring out the true personality of an individual. There are those who say, "That was not him talking; it was the alcohol." They are wrong. The alcohol strips the individual of inhibitions and reveals his layers of masks. It is then that the psychic center of the person is revealed unclad to all viewers. It is then that we are justified in judging the quality of that person.

***

Historians contradict one another. We cannot read of the past without encountering dispute. So, in frustration, we ignore history as mere gossip on the street. Thus the past becomes as obscure as the future. We then tend to repeat our errors. The intrusions by The United Stares into Vietnam (1946-1975) and Iraq (2003) combine as examples of our ignorance of history.

***

We coddle and tutor and struggle to make the world better for our children. When they grow older and have their own children, they might tell them of their own youth. They might then speak of "The good, old days", with nostalgia.

***

Please do not forgive me too quickly or too easily or too soon. It makes me feel even more guilty. Perhaps that is why you do it.

***

When I first began to read subjects of my choosing, I read Melville, Poe, Wilde and H. G. Wells and a bit of Shakespeare. Then it was off to the movies: the chief repository of dreams; a haven for the idle boy; now too busy to read. Then on to reflection, my thoughts turning inward, and forays into the world of myself. A binge of self indulgence. Today I write notes, reflections, observations about myself. I talk to myself, I write to myself and things are beginning to make sense. Too late in life for remedial action but plenty of time for reflection. There is still time to repent and atone.

***

Do not ask God for anything. If He wants you to have it you will get it; if not then not. He knows best what you should have and you know nothing.

***

"There is properly no history, only biography"
R. W. Emerson (1803-1882)

It is with respect that I diverge from the above view. History is the result of many factors and only occasionally shaped by man. It is the vanity of man that causes him to exaggerate his importance to history. To the extent that man has impacted upon history, he himself has been shaped by his environment. History is more the product of geography, seismology, climate, topography, plate tectonics, oceanography and other aspects of the dynamic of our planet. The history of the vast and diverse United States could not have happened in a small island in the Pacific or a village in the Arctic. The awe inspiring history of Egypt could never have occurred without The Nile River. Mountains and oceans have isolated cultures, each with their own peculiar history. The planet is our home, our battlefield, our playground, workplace and cemetery. The planet dictates our history and even now emits signals of our future.

"The land does not belong to us. We belong to the land."
Chief Seattle (1786-1866)

***

The mother's identification with her child may be so complete that she treats her grown children as though they were still infants. To the extent this is true it is understandable. For if the children are indeed not yet full adults then perhaps the mother may still be in her youth.

***

Few dispute history as written by noble scholars. Over time they seem generally to agree what happened in the past. Who can argue with the prognostications of the futurists, for they tell us of what might be in a distant tomorrow. It is the stories of today that are generally in dispute.

***

Avoid a man who claims to have all the answers. I prefer to listen to an honest man who admits he has no answers. I will gladly walk beside this man as together we search out, uncover and decipher the Truth.

***

The only thing sadder than divorce is staying together when one or both wants to end the marriage. Face facts and move on.

***

All the wonderful adventures of history pale beside the Great Adventure upon which we all have lately embarked: the adventure of life itself.

***

When the victorious general meets with his defeated foe, they both weep. The dead and the maimed of both armies demand it. For these men victory and defeat are but two sides of the same, bloodied coin.

***

We both wished that our young passion might have lasted forever. The taste and fury of our lust are still fresh upon our lips and deep within our memories. Time passes and passion transposes into affection. We have become close friends and faithful, gentle lovers. We two are as one. We are in love.

***

Forgive the greedy skinflint who counts his wealth by night and spends his pennies grudgingly. His childhood was certainly more sad and empty than your own. Your smile might be the only one he sees today.

***

A triangle in architecture is most stable; it does not "rack" or swivel at its corners. It stabilizes everything from bridges to spaceships. A triangle in the structure of love can result in broken homes, dead bodies and orphans. It makes for great drama. A triangle in love will always distort lives.

***

A male mallard duck and a jet airliner intersect (5000 feet apart in altitude), right over my house. The airplane has been around for about one hundred years; the duck for over a million. Planes have changed their design hundreds of times in one hundred years: ducks not once. Man needs a vehicle to fly: the duck does it alone. There are no passports for the duck, no luggage, no clothes, no compass, no schedule, no boundaries, no fear of heights, no in-flight movie he has seen before, no body cavity searches: just the stars and the winds and a watery place to land and rest. He winters down South and summers North on this river. The pilot of the plane carries a pistol now and passengers fear terrorists. The colorful mallard duck glides gently on the water, his egg laden mate close astern.

***

The wisest men I have known were each, indeed, a fool for something: women, booze, gambling, fishing, hunting or golf. I was a fool for everything. Thank God I have achieved decrepitude and thus set aside my vices.

***

Without God, whom do you thank for your parents? Whom do you thank for the nation in which you were born? Whom do you thank for your wife? Whom do you thank for the thriving of your children? Whom do you thank for winning when all the odds were against you? How do you repay Him for these gifts?

***

It is difficult for a man to find a woman with whom he can be merely a friend. His libido interferes with such an arrangement. As he gets older, the prospect becomes more appealing; less stressful, complicated and tiring.

***

Certainly Eve tasted of the apple. Certainly Adam followed suit. What did God expect? That they might throw the apple at the snake? God planned it all!

***

When language fails us, when we reach out for adjectives and adverbs to define our feelings and find all words sterile; when we feel at one with the abstract, we are experiencing an epiphany. Let it transpire in a climate of silent awe. "**epiphany:** A comprehension or perception of reality by means of a sudden intuitive realization: *"I experienced an epiphany, a spiritual flash that would change the way I viewed myself"* (Frank Maier)." A.H. Dictionary.

***

It has taken me seventy years but I have learned how to dream pleasant dreams. When I am asleep and a nightmare creeps into my head, I simply wake up. I think of happy times and doze off. I sleep again in a world of wondrous dreams. I dream new myths and gain new victories. I sink long putts.

***

Ideally the writer writes for himself. If the product sells then that disseminates his work and puts coins in his pocket. If not, well, at least he had the dedication, courage, belief, and industry to write. To write solely for money is simply to have a job. Prostitutes, assassins and lobbyists have a job.

***

"Science commits suicide when it adopts a creed". T. H. Huxley
Theology commits suicide when it invades the science class. JCC

***

Religious writings are based upon the assumption that there is a personal God. Who will write a book about the path toward moral virtue that contains no ethereal presuppositions? There are hundreds of such books which can be found in the Philosophy section of the library.

***

When I was married things were different. If I saw a lovely woman at a party or in a store, I could not remark about her beauty to my wife for she would view such as a threat to our marriage. If I saw that same woman represented in a painting my wife and I might agree that here was, indeed, a classic beauty. I learned to keep quiet and steal a look or two. Now I walk up to that woman and say, "You are certainly beautiful!" She knows this, of course, but is always happy to hear a reaffirmation. I do not like women very much but some of them are truly stunning.

***

In the film classic *The African Queen* (1951) actress Katharine Hepburn, portraying a religious zealot, delivers the following line: "Nature, Mr. Allnut, is what we are put in this world to rise above." (This comment is subject to revision as we see a bit later in the film.) Nature is that power under whose nurturing hand we are allowed to thrive. Nature is the system which we either love and understand or in which we become irrelevant and extinct. Nature is a nurturing Mother or a stern Father, depending upon our behavior. Religion is the intruder which Nature must learn to tolerate.

***

I often wonder why it is that music, of one sort or another, has such a general appeal. Why is it "the universal language"? Is the rhythm the memory of mother's heart beat? Is the melody the familiar sound of the wind or the birds in the trees, or the tittering of the swollen brook? Is it then the sound of thunder or the thunder of a great waterfall? Why play music? Why pay to listen in silence to the roar of the symphony or the whisper of the solo harp? Will I someday learn the answer or simply listen in pleasure and wonder?

***

I have watched as the "lower" forms of life demonstrate constant, common sense. Migrant birds spend the winter nearer the equator. Lions kill and eat the slower gazelles; (the gazelles evolve more speed). Butterflies perform their important task with colorful enthusiasm and earthworms come above the ground in time of flood and burrow back in when things dry out. Only Man seems often to act against his own nature; as though he possessed no inner compass; acts out the dictates of his self-destructive demons.

We humans fight more wars in the name of our religions and our ideals than we do to protect our sovereign territories. We forfeit more lives on the altar of our beliefs than did the ancient Aztecs in their blood-spattered temples or Torguemada in the fifteenth century Spanish Inquisition.

***

Man among the mob is another man. Picture one hundred men gathering together in a remote field. Now depict each man masked and each wearing a similar garb covering his entire body. Add a fiery speech urging them on to action. Their uniformed appearance has achieved a synthesis of the group and hidden faces have provided anonymity. Now anything can happen.

***

A carpet of blue-green grass, punctuated here and there by dandelions, is a sight to warm my heart. It is not my carpet or yard or field. Ah, the relief! I own no lawnmower nor will I ever. I have bushes and trees and gravel and large rocks. I have wildflowers and flowering bushes. I too have dandelions but I allow them to live out their lives in peace. I do not rip them out nor gleefully poison them like some do. I am a naturalist. Let nature surround my house! I get to sleep late while others toil. That has always been my fond ambition.

***

If there would have been slow motion movies four hundred years ago we could have then been able to better study the flying motions and techniques of various birds. Then we would have had a flying machine three hundred years ago instead of one hundred years ago. One invention often enables a score of others to be brought forth.

***

The entire family crowds together to watch the baby take his early steps. Arms outstretched to hold his balance he lurches from couch to coffee table; four full steps! Perhaps a party is in order. Imagine then how proud the birds are to watch their young ones take to flight. No wonder they sing.

***

Very few of our fatherly admonitions to our sons will be acted upon by the young men. It is in their nature to ignore what is said and learn most things the hard way; that is by experience. Perhaps this is best, for learning by experience far outstrips mere obedience to advice. Experience is not only the best teacher, it is the most demanding and least forgiving. No father would instruct so harshly as does experience. But our words of caution are not lost. They will reappear out of the mouths of our sons as they raise their own boys.

***

There are more problems caused by laws than are caused by crimes. Criminal courts, judges, lawyers, policemen, prisons, parole officers, and millions of pounds of paperwork are required to apprehend, adjudicate, convict or acquit, sentence, then house, feed, medicate, and control millions of men and women in state, local and federal detention centers than can be justified by any standard of "justice". And even capital punishment does not seem to stop murderers. Reason is as absent in our justice system as it is in anarchy.

***

For a man to be praised by his mother carries less weight as they both age. She will praise your every action and excuse your every fault. Hers is the blind adoration we seek in vain from our wives. All this is quite proper.

***

As a lad I was an avid reader of short stories. As a grown man and a writer I have discovered that there are few obstacles more intimidating than writing a short story. There is so much said; and said so succinctly.

***

Never correct or embarrass a man in the presence of his wife. He will not forgive you. Neither will she.

***

It is an axiom of a democracy that: "Justice delayed is justice denied." This is so as long as "justice" does not include capital punishment. To the death row inmate, justice must be painfully reviewed; delayed by the appeal system in order to avoid yet another, unjust murder. The thing about every murder is that it cannot be undone.

***

I watch many movies. There are a myriad of wonderful scenes and memorable quotations in the films I've seen. I sometimes quote them from memory (to myself) when they seem appropriate. There is now released "The Dictionary of Film Quotations" (Crown Trade Paperbacks N.Y.C.). It is stocked with 6,000 of them. In the movies they let you finish a sentence.

***

Exactly one hundred years ago man experienced powered, winged flight. Now we have the spaceships, the Moon Walk and the artifical island we call The Orbiting Space Lab. We send a mechanical scout to Mars. Intrepid men and women have died over these one hundred years: Test pilots, Air Mail pilots, airline pilots and their passengers, Warriors, Cosmonauts and Astronauts. Birds have been flying for millions of years. They have not evolved as fast as humans. They have not needed to.

***

In certain regions around the Arctic Circle, the crime of murder was punishable by death but was totally forgiven if the act was committed in a fit of passion. This reprieve was bestowed only one time; a second event resulted in prompt execution. To me this makes sense. The laws of simple cultures are usually quite simple and almost always just.

***

A belief in God and His justice and an afterlife that rewards and punishes is as old as civilization. God will take care of the innocent and mete out final justice to the guilty. Such belief can justify the comment voiced by a advocate of "law and order" who, in complaining of the amount of appeal time and the money it takes to execute a convicted man, uttered: "Kill them all and let God sort it out!"

***

Encouragement. Ridicule. Spoken by the father, the coach, the teacher or society, the one can help foster a champion or a President. The other can create an angry coward or a lifetime convict.

***

There are those leaders who would rather engage in a war (sending others to die) than apologize and those who would rather lie than admit error.

***

One may watch a clown and the comedic actor but must *listen* to the "stand-up", stage comic. He tells us the truth with only slight exaggeration and let's us see the world through the slightly distorted lens of his personal, ironic vision. Our response to him is the laughter of recognition.

***

If you undertake the vocation of your choice you will excel. Love the work you do and your life will be joyful. Financial rewards may well follow as the quality of your work improves. You will cultivate an inner peace. And should you die penniless, you will have died doing the work you love.

***

A good memory is a blessing or a curse, depending on what you have to remember. Accumulate your memories with care.

***

My nervousness is the result of my awareness of myself. I dread appearing nervous and it shows. Failing in the attempt to break the cycle causes me anxiety. Thus I stay hidden; always on the brink of disappearing.

***

Movies are my weakness and my passion. As I often moved about when a youngster I found movies to be a constant in my life. From one town to the next the new movies were playing and the old films, (the best of the lot), were the same for me wherever I lived. And now, so many years later, I watch the films of my youth and I am young again. I find new delights in old movies: things I had missed or misunderstood years ago. The list of my favorite movies is longer than all the roads I have traveled. I am lost in the moving pictures.

***

When a young couple falls in love, each for the first time, they believe that they are the first ever to have had such feelings. Isn't that wonderful?

***

In the arts, some are able to imagine and construct new forms. Others work more successfully within pre-configured structures. I think it does not matter what one creates as long as he or she is able to express an idea that leaps across time and distance into the open mind of another.

***

Life insurance is expensive. What might a life assurance policy cost?

***

The memories recalled by an old tune have the charm of the present. The color of her dress, the breeze of her breath upon your neck, the sweat of two hands clasped together, the strains of the music and her laughter: all these come rushing upon you from fifty years ago. Old songs have magical powers. Memories are as real as this paper.

∗∗∗

Effects are obvious; they shine like beacons in the darkness. Causes are obscure; they secrete themselves in the fathomless past. They are sometimes causes of other causes. Cause and effect. I get confused.

∗∗∗

My learned friend was ashamed of his illiterate family background and it embarrassed him further that he was so embarrassed.

∗∗∗

Many years ago, a cynical friend and I were discussing the state of popular music. He summed up his opinion with these words: "Ninety percent of popular music is junk." I was at first shocked, then moved to ascribe the comment to his misanthropic view of the world in general. Then I thought more. Of the hundreds of songs that made it into the top one hundred sellers of ten years ago, or two years ago, or last week, only several remain today "popular". The "popular" is made to sell. The product does not *precede* popularity but *follows* the whim of the mob. Rock concerts are not music so much as they are shows. A "Top Forty" radio station changes its play list *every day*. If a test of art is its longevity, we can forget about popularity as a component of quality. For me, the test of art is indeed the test of time. It must hang on from year to year and generation to generation. Enjoy the passing fad and dance to the current beat but do not yet call it art.

∗∗∗

All my lies are catching up to me at once. Now they close in like so many assassins ready to carve me. I must lie my way out of this mess in a hurry!

∗∗∗

Of all the paintings I have seen, I can remember only oval frames or those with four ninety degree corners. Am I missing something or have the artists neglected other plane shapes?

∗∗∗

When the children were small they needed so many things from me. I complained to myself and my wife about the time taken from my labors or my play to look after the needs of my children. Now the youngsters have grown. They require nothing from me now. It is painful not to be needed.

***

We make such fools of ourselves when overcome by our primal need to reproduce our species. I see that the scientists may soon produce a human baby by cloning; in a test tube, I am told. I wonder if we men and women will act more sensibly then; become more reasonable; less passionate. I hope not.

***

Late at night, when the whole world seems asleep, I think of the past and what might have been if I had been wiser, if I had been kinder or been more attentive to those whom I loved and who loved me. Sometimes a night-long depression bears down upon my soul and I wakefully dream of the death within my reach. I hope it may be soon so that I can find relief from my relentless, racking memories. I struggle for control. Then the first light of dawn and the first song of the bird and I am once more glad to see another morning. Perhaps it will be a good day. I must stay alive to see it.

***

I was in a distant city for a two-week vacation. I met some interesting, happy people, natives to that nation, and we became great friends. They tried to talk me into remaining with them for a few more weeks. Simply change my hotel reservation and my return flight and loaf for a while in the sun, listen to the music and watch the ocean and the birds. But I had things to do. I said goodbye and left at my scheduled time. I wish now I'd had the good sense to act less sensibly. That regret occurs often to us all.

***

It is easier to understand every card game ever devised than it is to discern the complexities of a woman's mind.

***

Have you ever thought that your neighbor earns too much money for the work he does? Then ask yourself if you would do his work for his pay. If so, then learn his trade and join his profession. If not, then turn your mind to other matters.

***

DROPS OF WATER, GRAINS OF SAND

In searching of the ultimate cause, The Uncaused Cause, I usually find either God or The Big Bang. These do not satisfy me. I struggle to become my own first cause. It is a lonesome task and I sometimes feel lost in my own skin.

***

It is possible to be in love and keep it a secret from the whole world: even from the object of your love. It often makes sense to hide love. I adored a younger lady for six years and never said a word or exhibited a gesture that would reveal my feelings. She was much better off without me in her life. I felt secure and happy that I was in love and no demands were being issued by either party. She is gone now. I will never see her again. I know that I will always be in love with her. She had green eyes and a soft voice.

***

I simply adore cats and dogs. No sense explaining why. Those who understand know why and those who do not do not. Pets are the only thing I revere which I will never again wish to own. It is not that they are too much trouble but that they all die too soon. They end up breaking my heart.

***

In the 1960 movie *Psycho*, the deranged, fatherless character Norman Bates says a line which has stuck in my mind: "A mother is a boy's best friend." At first this seemed to be understandable if not true, but the more I thought about it the more uneasy I became. The film deserved a second look, the line; a serious study. Mothers usually find no fault in their sons. They blindly worship their boys. "Everyone is out of step but Johnny!" These are the words of the uncritical mother. Such coddling is not the function of a friend or a father. The young son often tries to displace the father as center of the mother's life. If the father allows this, or if he should die, the natural order of things is disturbed. A normal growing boy begins to move (at about puberty) from his mother to his father for emulation and guidance. Norman never had or sought a male model. Under certain circumstances the mother/son relationship can become a disaster. *Psycho* was indeed the proper place for that unusual line. It was meant to be disturbing and it was.

***

In a few days my eldest granddaughter will graduate from high school. If her summer vacation is anything like mine was, some fifty years ago, it may well be more than memorable; it may be life altering. God, protect this child from herself and please furnish her with a lad who values her companionship.

***

As our parents fretted about us, we now worry. Justice, thou art blind and cruel!

***

I am a fault finder. I learned this from my parents who so often found fault with me. They were merely trying to perfect me, I know. Yet they wore me down. (I became the same perfectionist with my own children.) I always loved Mom and Dad. I am still as imperfect as they. I came to understand them and now that they are gone, I miss them both. They taught me manners and grammar and now, from afar, without a word, they teach me love.

***

Very few men find happiness or satisfaction in either fame or fortune. When these are garnered they are but the unintended consequences of hard work being performed by those who love the work and therefore excel. Excellence is what they seek and slavish persistence is the price they yield up in order to attain it. Notoriety and money are merely by-products of the mastery. A man must approach his work as to an altar; he comes to sacrifice, not to solicit. He bears an offering not a petition.

***

In my life I have known five women for whom I would have given my life had it been required. I knew them all in my twenties. Thank God not one of them ever needed my life to be forfeit or I might not have ever met the others. Now I would not give a dollar for a house full of them and they not a cent for me.

***

Romantic love is meant for the young, the fertile and the strong. Raising children will be their lot and their joy. Yet, since obtaining a solid education can take till he is twenty-two or more, and there must then be time to flirt and court and choose and be chosen, a proper man can get married only at about twenty-seven or thirty. He will be too old to skip rope with his grandchildren.

***

An act which may seem shocking to us at fifteen will seem acceptable at twenty-five, normal at forty-five, commendable at fifty-five, amazing at sixty-five and impossible at seventy-five. From then on, it would again seem shocking. Whatever it is, do it while you still can!

***

We were each a burden to our parents from the moment we were conceived until we left home to make a place of our own. None of us wants to become a burden again to anyone. Therefore we must prepare against any and all eventualities that might cause us to become a burden to our children.

***

The paws of a raccoon are as sensitive as the lips of a human. He browses through the shallows of the local creek, searching for food, using only those front appendages while he gazes about for predators. On my porch he picks through the dish of berries, nuts and grapes and selects the items he wants, using only his front paws. He looks at me through the window of my office. He is my friend and I am his. It is three AM and we are both busy. I wave at him. He stares at me while he selects items to his taste. I place my two hands above my keyboard and begin selecting words.

***

Every hematologist knows that blood type Group O Rh neg. is the "universal donor " and blood type Group AB Rh pos. is the "universal recipient". This rule is a generality subject to certain regulations and exceptions. So, in procreation, man is the universal donor and woman the universal recipient: a generality also subject to certain regulations and exceptions. In the latter case, it is best if the donor and recipient are acquainted.

***

The overthrow of a tyrant is usually followed by a period of anarchy. When the looting and blood bath subside, a new government is formed and, with luck, peace reigns within the nation. Then greedy eyes turn outside; gaze with envy at the peaceful neighboring state which thrives. Conquest brings booty, glory, hubris and welcomes the next leader who, by natural law, will become the forebear of the next tyrant. The tragic struggle is replayed. We learn nothing. Perhaps this is the way of natural selection: mindless, careless evolution.

***

The young man next door plays his recordings so loudly as to shake my windows. I complained to him once. He politely agreed to be quieter. He continues to blare the mindless songs even on a Sunday morning. He reminds me of myself at that age: careless and self absorbed. I shall buy ear plugs and let his parents struggle with him.

***

There is a time for action, be it positive or negative, pro or con. There is also a time to do nothing. Pause. Wait. Think. Let the world spin a bit and see what comes up. Relax. Then, when performance is again called for, you will be rested and ready for action.

***

When I hear a prayer from the pulpit beseeching God to protect our troops in this or that war, I see another priest in another temple praying to the same God for the protection of his nation's warriors: our enemies. I wonder what God must think. Perhaps He favors one country over another. Perhaps he doesn't care. Maybe he is busy with other matters. Who is in the right? How do we know? How does God decide? My head clouds up and I just stop thinking and join the congregation in prayer.

***

If God didn't expect laws to be broken he wouldn't have made so many of them. Then the Catholic Church added seven or eight more and other Christian Churches added others, then the Moslems and their dress code and the Hindus with their cows and the atheists with their law suits and on and on. No wonder most folks walk around with only slightly repressed guilt complexes. We can hardly get through the day without a sin. Thank God for forgiveness; otherwise Heaven would be a very lonely place.

***

A facility with foreign languages is a gift. It can be used only after it is unwrapped. Learn another language and see if you are among the lucky ones who grow to new dimensions when bilingual. If so, learn yet another.

"To learn another language is to gain another soul." (Anon.)

***

During courtship a woman pretends that she understands and agrees with every peculiarity of the man she will wed. After the proper number of children have been born and she tires of his affection, she then begins to demand understanding and claims not to be receiving it. She retreats into herself bringing with her as many of the children as she can. She, who has never understood and never wanted to understand him, claims that her husband no longer understands her. The truth is that they never understood each other and neither ever cared to. They were drawn together: he to her body and she to his bank account. This is how the world works for the betterment of the species.

***

There is more gambling in a marriage than there is in a casino. More people play at the former than at the latter. While one may lose money in the casino, a more valuable commodity may be obliterated in the angry home: the mind.

***

Today is June 1. There is a frost warning! Has Nature been smoking some potent, new weed? The flowers are shocked. Even the weeds dive for cover. The hummingbird hides or, perhaps, he has gone back to Louisville for a few days. I have a foot warmer fired up in my workplace. I am bewildered by this aberration. Did I fly to Alaska last night? Perhaps the Planet has turned upside-down while I napped! That seems the most probable answer.

Which reminds me: I have lived in Florida, near the Ocean, where the warm breeze brings forth the fragrance of the night-blooming jasmine while the scantily clad girls on the noonday beach turn my mind toward "impure thoughts". I have floated through The Everglades and seen the beauty of the brutal hand of God in the bright plumage of a thousand birds and the bulging eyes of the alligator. I have watched the sun rise over the Atlantic and seen the great flotilla of yachts from Key Largo to Palm Beach. I longed for Indiana and Michigan and home. Now I am home. I will not yearn for another place.

***

Divorce is the willful murder of a marriage. Or it is the mercy killing of a sick animal. Or it is the breaking of a promise or the keeping of another obligation: to one's self. It is a Hobson's Choice placed upon the children: agonizing pain as they suffer the division of loyalties. Or is it a release for them from a life of tension; living in the center of the battlefield? Does it suck them down into the blackness of a maelstrom? It is lawful but breaks the law of "vow" upon which all laws and unions are based. It is a sad release from a sad situation. Each is now free to do as they will but still the captive of glorious memories that can never be reclaimed. The process, painful by design, leaves scars upon every victim. Let no union be torn apart without the frightening sound of ripping, screams of agony and the shedding of remorseful tears. Let us pray for them all. Give them the wisdom to mend or the courage to survive. Please, God, please do not forget them.

***

Is it so strange that I would be made sad by the sight of a dying oak tree in my wooded lot? I think of the winters he has seen and the birds he has helped raise. I wonder how many thousands of squirrels he has sheltered and the leaves he has provided for shade. I think of how tall and straight he was and how proud. I wish I could help him now. I will not cut him down but let him fall when he is ready. The winds and the ice and time itself will determine the date. Yet he did live. Old men and old trees understand these things.

***

The world moves too quickly. It changes. People change. The woman for whom I would have given my life (and to whom I gave my living) was perfect for me. Then, instead of dying, we lived on and both she and I changed. We are no longer together. I would seek her out and again pledge myself to her but we are forever altered. We are not what we used to be.

***

An ample lump in my wife's belly turns to a toddling squealer who amazes us as he learns to walk, then to talk and then to become a small person. That is how fast it seems to happen. Then school and playtime, college and women and then a marriage with three lovely grandchildren all amid his productive labors; and hers. Now I am no longer needed. I think of the past and tell the children of the past and they must think that I live in the past. But it is thoughts of the future that fill my mind. Their future is the subject of my thoughts and my work. I think of my grandchildren and remember their father and my father and suddenly I have over one hundred years tumbling about in my head. I want to tell of the past to help inform their future. I bore them.

***

If your adult child seeks your counsel, respond with facts and examples from your own experience. Point out pitfalls and supply several alternative actions from which he may choose. Avoid direct instructions. Let him decide. Grant him the power of self-determination. Help him to grow.

***

My relics of the past are ignored as I write. When I am gone they will be sold by the pound or the box and no one will know how much they were coveted, but in the end, ignored by me. I have similarly ignored people whom I loved. For that I deserve a lengthy punishment after I die. But now I write. Tomorrow I will read and listen and phone an old friend for lunch.

***

I close the windows, draw the blinds, shut off the music and try to seal myself from distraction. But I cannot shut down my mind and its doors are wide open to destructive thoughts. That's the thing about the mind: it resists restrictions. It will wander where it pleases and now it pleases to torment me with thoughts of the past. I worry about the future. It is no time to write.

**

In the history of our planet there have been cataclysmic events that have changed the globe. Perhaps the arrival of Man was yet another such event.

**

When all the news is absorbed, all history is complete, when the secrets of Earth and all the planets and the knowledge of all the stars is written down and the very Universe is logged into a data base; when these things are fully known, Man will still ask, "Who am I?" and, "Where do I come from?" and "Where will I go?' and "Why?" These are Man's perpetual queries.

**

There was a time when your children needed your help even to bathe, walk, eat or dress. Slowly they became independent. One day you noticed that they seemed to be doing well totally without your help. Then there comes a new problem for them and you want to reenter their lives as facilitator, but this problem is now beyond your ability to assist. It is one of the sad realities of the world. You are ready, willing but unable to assist your child in matters that are his alone to solve. The fact that you are impotent in this situation surprises you. It saddens you.

**

Benign lies are often contrived to soothe fears or calm nerves or to imbue courage. We practice these on our comrades and they upon us. These are the type of lies we tell ourselves to help us confront the uncertainties of each day. They are good lies. How would we cope without them?

**

The child asks many questions of his parents. Most begin with "Why?" and continue for several years till we parents either lose our composure or run out of answers. The truth is that The Big Questions are beyond our ability to answer. The Important Questions defy our comprehension. So we contrive explanations. Thus are born religions and myths. They usually satisfy children and most adults. But, tell me, why *does* the grass grow green?

**

Drinking alcohol has several, small advantages and creates scores of problems. Among the negative aspects are personality changes, loss of friendships, alienation of loved ones, physical deterioration and death: including suicide. Or, the death of others through manslaughter, (vehicular or battery), and murder. Let two drinks last the night.

***

We all worship the Sun. Every plant, animal, mountain, sea and the very Earth owes its existence to the Sun. It is the source of all we know. It sets our clocks, tells our days and counts the numberless years. Those ancients who prayed to the Sun knew this. They learned their posture from the bowed heads of the phototropic flowers. Like all Gods, He forbids us to look upon Him with the threat of blindness. When we would see the Sun we must look at its mirror: the Moon. Earth gently tethers the Moon as the Sun holds the Earth. The Moon rules the tides and is a night-light to the traveler. It calls lovers together.

***

In world mythology, The Sun is both fearsome and the creator. It provides for us but can burn us in anger. Our life depends upon the Sun. The Sun is a man. The Moon is a gentler being; a woman. She neither scolds, threatens or punishes. Her light is a reflection of the Sun and is soft and quiet. Yet she can gently rule the ocean tides. Her moods are many. She is a shape shifter. Every twenty-eight days she hides from us for a period. How can we not love the moon? She is always either whispering a poem or singing a lullaby.

***

If every man and woman on Earth would act in accordance with the vows they take, the laws they approve and their generally accepted obligations, the World would indeed be a paradise. What power prevents this?

***

Religions embrace The Commandments, the basic laws of God, they say. Then their priests periodically interpret the laws, then design exceptions for each of them, then contrive a means for the expiation of sins by use of religious sacraments. Religion seeks to threaten us into submission, dictate our actions, define taboos, prescribe and describe punishments; threaten us with eternal fire if we stray from their teachings. They, like secular authorities, even offer us a reprieve if will plead guilty and offer forth defined regret and proper atonement. All this and they expect us to love the zealots who themselves are as wont to sin as we? God is angry at religion.

***

Over the years I have come to believe that Man is a stranger on this planet. Where he came from I do not know. His future survival here is in doubt. He either nibbles away or gobbles up his own nest, hunting grounds and recreational fields. He has the best brain on the planet and uses it to war with his brothers, rob his neighbors and slaughter other species into extinction. Sometimes I am ashamed to belong to that race. I am confused.

***

Although we do not normally use "love" and "attachment" as synonyms, we do frequently get them confused. For we may love one with whom we have little or nothing in common yet become attached only to those with whom we share a wide variety of agreements. Attachments are formed over time. Love can occur at first sight. If, over time, we are very lucky, we can become attached to one we love. Similarly we can begin to love one to whom we have become attached. A combination of the two states is close to perfection.

***

The study of causality leads either to a belief in God or a theory of Chaos. The search into the past to discover the "uncaused-caused cause" is futile. The cause of an effect is itself the effect of an earlier cause. The absolute, first cause of any event remains forever obscure.

***

The Ten Commandments, as I learned them, have varying interpretations. Their simple statements are open to discussion and debate today; some five thousand years after their presentation. The Clergy are the lawyers of these rules and clergy, like lawyers throughout the world, have rarely agreed upon anything. So we "sin", in part, for lack of an official, coherent, universally accepted reading of the law. For centuries we have slaughtered each other in the name of God! Beware. Someday God may simply abandon us.

***

A reappraisal of historic events is always in progress and it is always necessary. New information is constantly being discovered, de-classified and/or otherwise exposed in new publications. This is not "revisionist" in nature but merely the exposition of newly acquired facts. Revisionist appraisals are often reflective of history written by those who have private animosities or merely a book they wish to sell.

***

Today we are living in a history about which many books will be written. It is always so. We cannot see the ocean when we are swimming in it. We cannot see history when we are living in it. Our progeny will write of our lives from a great distance. We can only hope they will be fair. Better yet, compassionate.

***

In my library of Mythology there must be hundreds of gods. Over the centuries many of these deities have been shelved one by one. As we learn the natural cause of winter and summer, lightning and thunder, the gods fall into disuse. Neptune no longer rules the sea. Spring no longer needs a goddess; we have a calendar to clock its arrival. We've just about wiped them out, these old gods. Yet we do need God and Heaven and Hell and other antique beliefs to help us explain the as yet unknown aspects of our existence. Until Man understands himself we will need God's help. And Man is too busy to discover himself.

***

It is sad that publishers judge potential volume of sales in order to justify the printing of a book. In general, a book must have a wide appeal in order to garner the high volume of sale required to print and distribute a volume of literature. Thus, each book editor must look first at the salability of a manuscript and only then judge its quality, originality and usefulness to the community in general. The editors who are employed by publishers are everyday faced with that old choice between quality and quantity; between excellence and profitability; between the ideal and the practical. These people earn their keep.

***

For a warrior to succeed in battle, first two diplomats must fail at diplomacy.

***

In my advancing age I have learned to live without many things which, as a boy, I had sought and believed were within my power to obtain. In truth our wishes always outstrip our powers. That is why we call them wishes.

***

Closed doors are usually an invitation to stay out.. at least a signal to knock.

***

He who is not of two minds when dealing with any significant problem is not thinking: he is merely doctrinaire.

"Porgy and Bess" was produced as an opera in 1935, it was based on a book by DuBose Haywood of Charleston, South Carolina (1925). Haywood and his wife Dorothy would produce a play (1927) based on the book. George (music) and Ira (lyrics) Gershwin sought to create a "folk opera" from the work and collaborated with the Haywoods toward its completion. (Haywood and Ira collaborated on the lyrics to "Summertime" and "My Man's Gone Now".) The Opera was finally ready . It was well received in 1935. It was performed by The Houston Opera Company in the 1970s and the company took it to New York City where it won honors for the best musical of that year. Another production was released on DVD video in 2001. Aside from the fact that it is one of my favorite musical works, it lends itself to jazz, which is one of my favorite genres. It is little known that, by iron-clad contract, when performed on stage it must contain an all black cast. (There are always two white men included as *policemen*.)

So two *nouveau riche*, New York, Jewish geniuses and a couple rooted in The Old South unite to write an opera about poor black folks, cast it completely with blacks and the opera plays somewhere almost every night. While the play always moves me deeply, I am even more struck by the daring of all the collaborators in 1934 and the racial and ethnic strife in The United States which it has thus far survived. It has thrived in a racially fractured nation. It will outlive all the last racial divides.

***

A lie is a virus. It may be still-born or never live to yield another generation. It may find a suitable host and survive; thrive through many generations within that host and its progeny. It may find the opportunity to "cross" to another species and infest another multitude. Yet, like all living things, it will die: or simply pause for a time appearing to die. A lie does indeed have a birth but its death is never absolutely certain. The swastika and the burning cross can still be found by dedicated eradicators; still flourishing on willing, eager hosts.

***

My lover asks me why I love her. The truth is that I love her because she loves me so strongly. (What better reason? Why not the truth?) But I tell her what she wants to hear: "I love you because you are the only woman who ever lived whom I could ever love. You are the one for whom I, and all men, search. Others have settled for emulators. I possess the original. May I never lose you". That seems to seal the bargain. I wonder why she loves me. Really.

Humans will always fall short of their potential. The only One who attains His potential is God; and I often wonder if He get is right all the time.

***

Encountering the truth can be a life-altering event. To the adolescent: "You will not live forever". To the adult: "You have an incurable disease and have only weeks to live". Alternatively, "I am so in love with you, I cannot bare to be apart", or, "You have just won the State Lottery!".

***

The experience of finding "truth" in art, has a special effect upon me. I am always surprised and often moved to tears, and I thus embarrass myself. I am struck mute if called upon to explain my obvious emotion. In fact, I have the answer. I am startled to experience in art what I had only imagined in my artlessness. I experience a moment of validation: an epiphany. These are tears of both humility and gratitude. Art takes a short-cut, from our senses to our cerebrum.

***

"Beauty" in a woman has its variations. First "in the eye of the beholder". But also there is a temporal aspect; a fluid fashion to which the woman must conform and which alters from time to time. Rubens painted a beautiful woman in the shape of a cherub. Today's fashion models seem to have only recently emerged from an internment camp in French Guiana. Perhaps the thing we call "beautiful" is subjective. Perhaps fashion is foisted upon us and our female partners by an industry; in order to make money. Could this be?

***

He was a boy of twelve when they buried his father, home from the war in Viet Nam; 1968. Tomorrow they will bury the ruins of his son, home from war in Iraq; 2003. They will lie side by side; two heroes now beyond pain. He will stumble on through an empty life with a scalded brain and two arrows in his heart.

***

Time is valuable because it is the only product of which we cannot obtain more. So the wealthy spend money to buy the time of others and employ them to perform time-consuming tasks. They thereby purchase time for themselves and the poor are allowed to subsist. An ideal arrangement.

***

If the same effort were expended in consultations and negotiations before the war begins as is dedicated to the arrangement of an armistice or the terms of surrender, wars would be rare indeed. More warriors would die abed.

***

I am often contradicted by my fellows in conversation. They are sometimes misguided in their arguments but I allow them time to press their case. I might learn something. Therefore I am not adverse to contradicting myself when reason prevails over passion. Reason is supported by fact. Passion is the child of fire. Both have a place in life but not the same place.

***

It was a brief war. Our overwhelming military superiority assured victory. We stated our motives for invasion. We then asserted more patriotic reasons. Now that the war is over we claim it was prosecuted for still other, even more obscure considerations. Our excuses varied; rescue, self defense, "freedom", "honor", but our cause was conquest. We wanted what they had.

***

A Tavern Near the Outer Banks of North Carolina. Late Evening:
December 16, 1903
"Them two brothers from the bicycle shop are still tinkerin' with that flying machine. Dreamers. God never meant for man to fly. That's for the birds. You'll never get me on one of those things. There's too much dreamin' goin' on. Loafers they are; crazy, lazy loafers. Why don't they get about their real work? They'd do better to tend to their families and raise up kids. Why, next thing they'll be saying' they're gonna fly to the moon! You wanna know what's wrong with this country? Too many dreamers! Elsie! Another round over here! Yep, that's the problem. Too many dreamers."

***

In conversation we allow breaches in the laws of our language. (Even the French acknowledge and permit both conversational and written language!) But when we write we must utilize a dictionary, a thesaurus, an encyclopedia, a Bible and other research material. We can forget, revise or deny what we may say but that which we write is testimony.

***

Sometimes, when the black mood is my master, I brood over what seems then to be an absolute fact: Every significant invention, every scientific breakthrough eventually develops into a weapon for killing our own species in war. Like the moon, I too have my dark side.

***

Black and white movies were the norm when I was a boy and color films were always very expensive to produce. I am told that today it can cost more to make a black and white film than to produce it in color. I like both formats. So does Hollywood. Long after color was dominant in Hollywood the following were produced in black and white: *On The Waterfront* (1954), *Touch of Evil* (1958), *Psycho* (1960), *The Pawnbroker* (1965), *In Cold Blood* (1967), *Raging Bull* (1980), *The Elephant Man* (1980), *Rumblefish* (1983), *Ed Wood* (1994), *American History X* (1998) and many more, all of which could have been made in color but the directors chose "b&w". In the history of movies there will always remain high honors for the great black and white films. Color is spectacular. Light and shadow is intimate. Color strikes the eye: monochrome the imagination. Study film. You'll see I'm right.

***

I now tell nothing but the truth. I am too old to have secrets. I lack the imagination and the sharp memory required to keep straight a string of lies.

***

I am armed and armored, visored and well horsed; prepared and poised for my enemies. Now, God, protect me from my allies!

***

"Reporting facts is the refuge of those who have no imagination."
(Marquis de Vauvenargues)
I think this fellow works in The White House or Congress. He used to write press releases for the film industry but he insists he finds government work more challenging. He earns a large salary.

***

On my first trip to New Orleans, Louisiana I found it to be oddly familiar. Of course, I had seen it depicted in films, both contemporary and historic, and read of its peculiar history, its fine restaurants, etc. Yet I was unprepared for the smells of food and flowers, the sights of St. Louis Cathedral, the above-ground cemeteries and the sounds of jazz. Every meal was memorable; every drink seemed made just for me. I wanted to stay. I did not want to return to our home on a lake in Michigan. It seemed to me that I was already home and wanted to stay there. Only the rationality of my wife helped me to pack and leave that city. I still believe that I belong in that fine hotel where the calls of the street vendors wake me and the merriment of the jazzmen lulls me to sleep.

***

We are born with the ability to reason and we crave intellectual order. Yet we continually find ourselves diverted by our basic passions. We seek to balance these two by claiming that our reasons are held passionately and our passions are, after all, quite reasonable.

***

Soldiers are trained for war. War consists of attacking the enemy and killing those who will not surrendered. Victory is the object of war. Policemen are peace keepers. They use force only when persons are in danger or in subduing unruly suspects. Having won a war, a nation sends in military police to maintain order, for soldiers are not trained for that mission. To use the warriors to keep the peace is like enlisting the tiger to mind the nursery.

***

Henry Clay once said: "I would rather be right than President". Are these two conditions mutually exclusive? It is true that in a democracy the *popular* fancy often defeats the *logical* fact but cannot one nominee be both?

***

For a student I'd rather have an ignorant child than a published professor. For carrying new wine provide me with an empty vessel.

***

In card games, like bridge, cribbage or gin rummy, luck is said to be king. But since luck, over time, is equally distributed we must conclude that, over time, it is skill and patience that triumphs. So luck calls itself "King" but skill rules the game.

***

As a child I used to visit the home of my mother's friend. I was always welcome there. On the dining room wall was a painting depicting a simi-nude, young woman playing a guitar. As a youngster I was curious to see a nude woman. A year or two later the picture became a source of lascivious thoughts. Later still it rose to the level of an ideal in womanhood. Then, over much time, I came to the realization that there are no *ideals*: merely women. Now, near seventy years of age, if I see that print in a catalogue, I merely remember my mother and that home and I flip on to other pages. Over time things do change.

***

Actor Gregory Peck died last night at age eighty-six. Within the last few months The American Film Institute voted Attucus Finch, as portrayed by Peck in *To Kill A Mockingbird* (1962), to be "America's Greatest Hero". He also took great pleasure in playing Dr. Josef Mengele, the Nazi butcher in *The Boys From Brazil* (1978). In that role he portrayed one of the history's most infamous villains. In an interview he chuckled that the role finally showed his range.

***

The only games worth playing are the games that are difficult to play and a struggle to win. Be it solitaire or golf, a team sport or a poker game, winning is merely the emblem. The money or the trophy are the booty of the raid. It is the contest itself and the memory of the battle that are the lasting treasure. One can spend the winnings, misplace the trophy and yet retain the pride that results from playing at your best. My best is all I have to give.

***

Sometimes it is desirable to write or speak the obvious. Otherwise, through disuse, the obvious may become obscure. The populations are ever evolving and old sayings are new to younger ears.

***

As a young man I was slender as a wire and some addressed me as "Slim". Over the years a sedentary life and a fine cook for a wife swelled my body into the shape of a dinner roll. My excess weight became a health hazard. I lost enough so that my waistline measured what it had been when people called me "Slim". Now these same friends tell me I look ill and fear I may be near death. I suppose I shall have to outlive them all and thereby show them their error.

***

We all hope that there is a God in Heaven and that He will ultimately forgive all our sins. But there is an Earth right here, with us, whom we do indeed know. When we sin against Her, She is slow, if ever, to forgive.

***

All men seek Truth. Of the few who believe that they have found it, there are those who call it "Law"; physical, religious and legal. Yet these truths change. History teaches us no lesson with more harshness and memorability than it teaches us the re-creation of "Truth". Therefore seekers of wisdom continue the search with minds wide open; ready for surprises. And still Truth forever sprints ahead of us, laughing, just beyond our reach.

***

Look about the world. See the powerful people pull all the strings. Kings, Presidents, Prime Ministers and Prelates use their powers and privilege to set the course and guide the ship of state. Yet everywhere it is the people who allow themselves to be pushed and pulled in so many directions. This, until revolutions erupt and anarchy prevails and executions become the order of the day. These events alter the political landscape. It is then that we know who rules. The people at first must allow themselves to be dominated. The people may then revolt and project their own power. Their world is washed clean for a time until the people voluntarily submit to a new order. In good times or bad, in democracies or monarchies, the people are forever sovereign. Therefore it is the people who are to be praised and they who are to be blamed.

**

We are taught that we should become "our brother's keeper". How far does this admonition extend? We speak of the "brotherhood" of man. Are the citizens of Iraq our "brothers"? If so, do we honor them by killing them and defiling their Holy Places and imposing our cultural values upon them in order to give them "Freedom"? Can Freedom be imposed from without? As individuals may enjoy freedom, they are restricted by laws from impinging upon the freedom of their fellows. A nation has freedom so long as it does not unduly disturb its neighbor. Citizens of one nation who are oppressed, (or who feel oppressed), have not only the right but the duty to themselves and to their children to revolt. Yet we need not urge revolution upon others. It will come in its time like a babe from the womb.

**

To write dialogue you must be of at least two minds, holding firm allegiance to both. Furthermore, you must keep your reader or audience in mind and remain true to the entire play which was conceived at the beginning. You must be of *three* or more minds. How do they do it? I do not know. No wonder some playwrights drink too much liquor or go crazy or both.

**

A bright, sun-filled day. A cool breeze from the north. Duties fulfilled. Dreams fresh in the mind. Plans for tomorrow. Your grandchild plays close by. A soft, gentle hand rests on your shoulder. Soon dinner will be ready. You can smell the smoky grill. Yes, this is a good way to live. This is a good way to die.

**

ı genre that is overly described and overly analyzed, but critics
ɔes often contain an element of moral ambiguity. The crimi-
ɛmpathetic and constituted authority is often flawed. A
be encouraged to believe in or agree with such notions, but
... allow a window for us to suppose. *Film Noir* is generally a
post-W.W.II phenomenon, when realism came into demand, and continues
to this time in twenty-first century cinema. It will remain because it contains general truths, self-revelations and morality tales. It is as realistic as a
photograph.

***

There are some cultures where beef is sacred and others where pork is
considered too filthy to eat. As a Catholic I was forbidden to eat meat on
Friday. Why this was so was never explained satisfactorily to me and,
indeed, that prohibition has been repealed some decades ago. I once had a
dog that would eat every table scrap presented to him except peas. When
given left-over stew he would attack it with gusto, wolfing it down: all but
the peas. He would lick each pea clean of gravy but never devour even one!
With him, I can only suppose it was yet another obscure, religious taboo.

***

earth spinning at 1000 m/p/h

"The mass of the earth is 6,000,000,000,000,000,000,000 tons, a
figure which transcends our power of imagination. Yet the sun is
333,000 times heavier, and its circumference is 109 times greater
than that of earth. No wonder it keeps the earth in obedience from a
distance of 93 million miles, although these millions upon millions
of tons of our globe are racing along with a speed of 18 miles per
second." *1080 per minute   64 800 per hour*
"The Oscillating Universe", Ernst J. Opik, (1960). *= speed of earth around sun*

This quotation makes me feel small indeed. Yet within each of our lives we
are great; central to our experience. I struggle each day to shape my world
into my own image and likeness but at night, with an ocean of stars (those
billions of other suns) spread out above me, I am reminded of my own,
relative insignificance and I relax. I glide into tranquillity. I sleep like an
innocent babe.

***

In mortal combat, we, who might otherwise swim, dance, play cards, eat
together or love one another, simply kill each other. Someday this war will
be over. Then we can resume profitable commerce and peaceful recreation.

***

All the laws of God and Man are designed to deter men from committing acts which, to that society in general, are abhorrent. These hated acts often come quite naturally to some men else there were no reason to prohibit them. The enactment of these laws is designed to restrict the rights of the individual in order that the general may be protected from the undesirable acts of the few. There are some cultures which allow acts that other cultures prohibit. There are cultures where a murder, when justly enraged, is totally forgiven: *once*. (A second such murder by the same person is punishable by immediate execution!). There is no law needed that prohibits my drinking from a putrid well or banging on my thumb with a sledge hammer. I am "free" to do these in a "free society". What is called "wrong" by society is often merely an "undesirable" misdemeanor or a "highly undesirable" felony. As the rights of a just society are rightly limited so then are the rights of the individual.

***

It is a common misconception that if history is written on high-quality paper and bound in leather it must therefore be true.

***

No matter what young lovers tell us, it is possible to love someone too much.

***

There are literally numberless books written on the life and times of U.S. President Abraham Lincoln. Each one claims to be revealing and truthful. Read them all and: you will be old, you will need glasses, you will suffer mood swings and you will know no more about Lincoln than you do today.

***

A lover is lost within a dream. Ungrounded, he is at the mercy of the winds. "She loves me. She does not love me. I need her to survive. Why did she not smile at me today? When can we be alone? Will she like my poem? She is the most beautiful creature ever set upon the earth. I can think of nothing but her!" God loves a lover and all lovers are to be treated as His lost children. They are temporarily insane. Marriage is the only certain cure.

***

A married man should not gamble at the casino. The weight of his domestic responsibilities bears down heavily upon his judgment and clouds his calculations; especially when the rent money is there upon the table.

***

There is no work of art to which the artist himself would not make at least a very small adjustment were he given the opportunity. The artist seeks perfection yet must also be prepared to settle for a close approach. He is never truly satisfied with his work. He turns away from his most recent creation and begins another. He once more seeks to become God. He fathers yet another child.

***

Even the old and infirmed have moments of enjoyment. They can be made happy in many small ways. I have heard some laugh with such enjoyment of the moment that they seem to have forgotten that they are mortal. Or, perhaps they laugh because they know that they are mortal.

***

People do not want to know the Truth. Truth is like the sun in that it throws light upon dark places. And Truth does finally reveal itself, though it be obscured by the thickest clouds or otherwise hidden from us, as the sun hides at night. The sun can blind our eyes and burn our bodies. The same truth that makes us wise is the truth that often shatters our dreams and deadens our hopes. But, after all, who truly knows the Truth?

***

Imagine a old sailor, a millennium ago, who plied the Northern oceans for a lifetime, employing the Northern Star as his chiefest guiding beacon. Now imagine he meets with a sailor from the South and is told of the constellation Southern Cross. Our old sailor will not believe. He will walk away from this heretic and seek out the company of other, Northern seamen: coreligionists.

Today The Southern Cross is depicted on both the New Zealand and the Australian Flags. (Epsilon, a fifth star, is included in the latter.) Things change. We learn slowly. Prepare for tomorrow. A new idea will become a fact and old ideas, books, flags and even religions will be subject to revision.

***

Armed with the best intentions, certain of your rectitude, eager to do good, you put your nose in where it does not belong. Shortly you'll have a broken nose and your fine resolutions be forgot.

***

A joke is often the truth, stretched out so far out of shape that you don't recognize it until it snaps back into your face. You laugh at the truth.

***

Of course we know that winning is not everything. There is losing. Losing at the proper time, in the proper situation, to the proper person may be the luckiest event in life. Losing can be winning if you gain an unsought prize.

***

No research scientist is a true theist, for his work is his God. He will spend more time in his laboratory than does a priest in his temple: more time in the pondering of his problem than does a pious monk in prayer.

***

We talk to communicate. We write to remember and to be remembered. Testimony in court is spoken but the stenographer records each word for posterity. The writer writes for all these reasons. He also writes in order to see today if what he wrote yesterday will make any sense tomorrow.

***

He studied and practiced, memorized, lived in the scenes, showed up to make up and wowed the audience. He got good reviews and praise from his peers. But that was not enough to keep him fed. He hungered for more. He surveyed the landscape and plotted his path. He learned how to get to the top. So he did what he did to get what he got and he gave what he got to us all. He was the actor. We were the audience. Together we made movie history.

***

All my grandchildren are perfect. Such flaws as they may have are like the slight imperfections in a hand-blown bottle, or the puff of white cloud in an otherwise azure sky, or a small, dark mole on the cheek of a fair maiden: merely accenting beauty.

***

From New York City to Baltimore to Atlanta to Miami, water soaks the earth. Rain has not fallen like this for over a hundred years. Out West is a drought. Many states explode into forest fires which swallow up houses by the hundreds and ignite trees into a million fiery torches. The East has extra water. The West needs water. Has no one ever thought of building a network of pipelines across this nation to move water from where it is flooding to parts where draught prevails? We have oil and gas pipelines. There is not enough money in water yet, I suppose. There will be.

***

If the Devil should ever attend a masked ball you can be sure that he will arrive wearing the mask of the devil. For, as all men know, a mask is designed to disguise the true identity of its wearer.

Television news. Nobody is getting it right anymore. The hosts on television are fashion models reading from a prompter. The words they read are written not by newsmen but by interested parties. Politicians are the mouthpieces of corporate or socio-economic interests. Therefore, I listen to music and read old books. If I ran this nation the way it should be run I would be impeached within days of my inauguration. So I shut up... mostly.

***

I have mentioned the animals that frequent my yard. I forgot to say how much each of them delights me; as though I were at a family gathering where nobody needs to be polite in order to know that he belongs.

***

I know many solitaire games. Over the years I have limited myself to those which are very difficult to win. Certain ones I almost never win but when I occasionally triumph I am happy for the entire day. Life is a solitaire game we never win but the playing of it can be exciting, each day new, challenging and even fulfilling. We know that we will lose in the end but we just keep on playing. Perhaps we are all victims of a fine addiction.

***

When he wears out and recognizes the limitations of himself and those about him, as he sees that perfection in merely an ideal established in his own mind by some mythological notion gone amuck: as he sees this, an obsessive man finally discovers that: "The good is superior to the perfect." (*anon.*)

***

Value is subjective. A trowel to a lawyer has no use but is invaluable to a mason. Light to a sculptor means nothing if he loses his shaping tools. So too, even money; cold cash, has a relative value. What one man spends on a taxi to take him to the airport can feed a family of four for a week in some cities. So men do not compare bank accounts. Your cash fortune is beyond my reckoning and my study, lined with books and unfinished writings, my freedom of thought, my right to be wrong; these cannot be bought at any price.

***

On the subject of absolute value I can think of no example. Even "absolute good" is often a matter of the culture in which we live. God, I suppose, is an absolute but by the time he has revealed Himself and His teachings to us, through the mouths and pens of His self-appointed interpreters, He is as obscure as the winds and as ambiguous as the seas.

***

A romance is like a beautiful aquarium. Sometimes it is good just to watch it; not try to improve it, over-plant or over-feed it. Let it develop as it may. Just leave it alone and enjoy it. Nature, when undisturbed, is a fine artist.

***

Over the many years of my life I have regularly renounced vices; one after the other, till now I am as prudent and pure as one can become. By sheer chance, the timing of these renunciations has coincided with my inability to practice them. I no longer drink all night. I quit chasing women, stopped swimming in the ocean, renounced climbing mountains and participating in bicycle races at the exact point in my life when these vices became too difficult for me to perform. What a fortuitous set of coincidences! I am a lucky man.

***

I disguise myself as a misogynist. But the truth is that women and I no longer attract. We do not get along as we used to. They have disappointed me and I them. I cannot think of a circumstance which would bring another woman into my life. They are happier without me and I am safer alone. And yet...

***

In lavish homes and public museums there are antique, ornately decorated vases that have never held a flower nor felt a drop of water.

***

There are so many languages in the world. One cannot learn them all. There are those who say that to learn another language is to gain another soul. I believe this to be true. Also, to learn one's own language, with all its shades and nuances, its permutations and combinations, its drama and humor and its multitudes of music; to do this is a lifetime adventure and worth the labor. Then to make it sing or weep is the writer's challenge. It is worth the effort and English is as good a language as any for that undertaking .

***

Of all the lessons we try to teach our children, one that is almost always omitted is the earnest instruction to them to become fully themselves. Each of us is unique and we have the DNA to prove it. It is our task to integrate that uniqueness into the general world which we inhabit. By diving into this mixture and mingling with society, we may add to the whole only by remaining unique. We each have something to offer and that thing is us. No one else can be us and we can be no one other than who we are. We can always do better and be better but we can never become another. To reflect upon our lives is the task of others. Our job is to live. We exist to complete the intricate mosaic of Man. That is our purpose, our duty and our joy.

***

Allies may not be friends. Friends may not be allies. The words are not synonymous. Your ally need have but one thing in common with you: you both have the same enemy. Should that enemy suddenly vanish, so may the alliance. History defines alliances. Your life identifies your friends.

***

The so-called: "I / It syndrome" consists of having an object or person cross your vision which you instantly realize you want, you need, without which you cannot live. There is an immediate connection between you and the object. Within seconds, you determine that you do indeed already hold title to it. Moreover, that you have always owned it. It has been yours from the beginning. It was created for you! Now the only remaining problem is to repossess your property and to make the re-acquisition complete, official and final. There was a painting in New Orleans and a woman in the local grocery. But this syndrome is more fully described in psychiatric journals.

***

Since before there was a word for war, men have been warring. And before each battle men from both sides pray for a swift victory with few casualties. How does God handle these contradicting prayers?

***

I know a lady, age thirty, who has five children by four different fathers and has never been married. She is a fine mother and a loyal friend. Once she cheerfully said to me, "I never planned for my life to turn out this way". I smiled and thought, "Often, even careful planning cannot overcome a careless nature." She is my friend. She never understood her own nature.

***

Nature uses wars to thin out the unfit and thus reduce the surplus population to a sustainable level. Nature has no moral standard, as those who perish in battle would tell us if they could. And what of the baby born dead, or the child struck down by a drunken driver? What of those lost to the careless tornado, cyclone, hurricane, tidal wave, earthquake or snow slide? Some deaths seem senseless to the thoughtful man. Yet they happen. Against large numbers, the value of one life diminishes. So we turn to God or become cynical atheists. And, finally, what is the difference?

**

"Situational morality" is a mode of conduct contrary to the teachings of organized religion, yet necessary and good when practiced in daily life to minimize pain and conflict. And situational morality is itself the mode of organized religions. The Christian Crusades, the Muslim Jihad; all the religious wars that ever were, are considered moral by those who prosecute them and sinful by those attacked. What must God think? How must He feel?

**

Lies are rightly considered wrong. Rightly used for the right reasons at the right time they are then considered "right" and "good". We practice flexible morality

**

In writing fact or fiction, for the masses or for few, my "target audience" is me. How could it be otherwise and still be honest? There are easier ways to cheat and steal. I write alone, in silence and with no certain reward. Like all writers, I have both something to say and a desire to be read. So I write.

**

A secret, once revealed, is no longer of import. Its usage diminished as it is broadcast across the land. When finally made public, secrets quickly change in value from diamonds to coal.

**

War and wealth. These two are related. Be they brothers, cousins or merely business partners, they are intertwined. Yet men will not willingly die in war for wealth. Therefore greed is disguised as "ideals" and many a peaceful man will die for an ideal. So off go the young warriors to their deaths while old men count their capital gains and women sew shrouds.

**

These priests, ministers, rabbis, mullahs, televangelists, witch doctors and soothe sayers; who are they to interpose themselves between me and God?

***

We mount a full scale, preemptive war and spend billions in order to achieve a "regime change" in another country. Let's not speak of morality. Why spend the money? Why spend the lives on both sides? Why disgrace ourselves in the eyes of history by striking first? We are told that one man is the cause of this war. If he must be removed, then why not simply use one of our many trained assassins? Oh, I forgot. That defies international law.

***

Choose your addictions with care, as you would your jailer or your chains.

***

To say, "I am unable to do that task." sometimes translates to, "I do not want to do that task." Even the lazy are energetic in their urge to avoid work.

***

Economics teaches that the more of anything an individual owns, the less value each unit has for that individual. I believe that theory is called, "diminishing marginal utility". So some spend ten million on a home, others one tenth of one million and others rent and still others go homeless. To some, one dollar means a meal. It is the same in war. If one hundred men are lost in battle, it is a horror; if ten thousand, it is a catastrophe, if 55,000,000 people are killed (total casualties, military and civilian, in WW II), it is a horror; a blot upon history. Yet as the numbers rise, the value of each individual diminishes. To each such individual his death meant every-thing. Be it one, ten, or 5000, the headlines are the same size.

***

Why is it that a couple married fifty years, never having been separated from each other for more than a day or two during all of that time; why is it that their memories of certain key events, mutually experienced, differ so widely? Selective memory? Individualized repression? An ever so slight difference in visual perspective? He is a businessman she a house wife? Listen as they contradict. All these things and more contribute to the lack of a unified view of the past. Memory is not reality. At best it is a subjective view of a past reality.

***

When Julius Caesar was killed a civil war ensued, reshaping the Roman Empire. When President Abraham Lincoln was assassinated the entire shape of Reconstruction was altered. Archduke Franz Ferdinand was shot and a World War erupted. (Who knew that his wife, Sophia, heavy with child, was also killed?) The assassination of President John F. Kennedy was an event that shocked the entire world. 58,000 American men and women were killed in the Viet Nam war. Do you know one by name? Clearly some people seem more important than others.

＊＊＊

To deny an error is to compound that error. Children are often guilty of this double infraction. So too are Churchmen, Congressmen, Police, Judges and Presidents. Recent history justifies the broadest application of this axiom.

＊＊＊

Political and religious arguments at social gatherings are generally discouraged. They are sometimes vociferous and never resolved. Such discussions between close friends are rare, *especially* when the two have differing views. Their friendship does not rest upon their agreement regarding politics or religion but on more important aspects of life. To the extent that an associate contends with you about politics or religion, he is testing his own argument, hoping to defeat you thereby to reinforce his own beliefs which have, of late, become suspect in his own mind.

＊＊＊

When the Earth quakes people flee, as fast and as far as they can. When a man falls in love with a woman he lingers close to the source of peril. The Venus Fly Trap is well named. Men and women are both well scripted by Nature. Reproduction of the species is a universal law.

＊＊＊

As humans we share 95% of our DNA with the African Chimpanzee. We learn our native language, our culture, our values and our morality from our parents, teachers and associates. We learn from experience and error. We all are the products of these environments. Yet somehow we remain unique. It is a miracle. We are not our parents or our brothers or our sisters or even our identical twin, with whom we share a perfect DNA match. We are unique. Perhaps it is through our fantasies and dreams that we humans experience our individuality. Maybe it is our refusal to give up our hopes and illusions. Maybe it is by retaining these devices and acting upon them that we are able to express ourselves upon our world. I know that there will never be another me.

＊＊＊

The remark, "I could tell you but then I would have to shoot you.", often attributed to National secrets, is told as a joke, but, since all jokes contain small truths, there is truth here. A State secret has value to the State as long as it is cloaked. When laid naked it becomes embarrassing to the State, valuable to all enemies of the State and often shocking to its peaceful citizens.

***

In the United States the very poor receive health services from a Federal program called Medicaid. Today Medicaid announced that it will no longer pay for circumcision of newly born boys. Often a cultural option, the procedure is deemed "cost prohibitive" and will be discontinued. Meanwhile a large tax reduction is newly in place which favors the very wealthy. Fresh from a war in Afghanistan, we now undertake a costly war in Iraq. I am ashamed.

***

Each parent stands ready to die for its child. For humans this opportunity rarely presents itself. In truth we die, soon or late, from our vices: sloth, anger, war, greed, insatiability. These and aging. Thus, do we yield the world to our children.

***

To tell you of my life would take a lifetime. Therefore I edit. In so doing I omit. This saves your time and my ink. Yet, no matter how devoted to truth I may be, it is in these very omissions that the truth may reside. In fact, it is in the very living of my life that my autobiography often lies. Who can read it? Only I, through a clouded prism.

***

The Children's Crusade of 1212 A.D. was a horror. From Germany and France they proceeded to The Holy Land to recapture sacred sites from the infidels. They all died along the way or were captured and sold into slavery, never to view their objective. Old men sent their children into battle for an idea. Shame upon the craven fathers who survived. God bless the brave children who died.

***

The games I win I declare to be games of skill. The games I lo\ose are, to me, games of mere luck. Thus I retain my self-esteem; win or lose, and thus I continue to play. Thus I live with joy as I play the game of life.

***

To lose one's mate through inattention; carelessness, is the most unforgivable of sins for which the punishment begins immediately and almost never ends.

**

Opinions may differ but facts are unequivocal. Therefore never argue about a fact which can be, or has been, proven. Prove it again or look it up.

**

Respect and *fear* are words not synonymous. Yet, in life, they often manifest themselves simultaneously, sometimes allowing these two emotions to become indistinguishable. We respect and/or fear: Fire, Stormy Seas, Priests, Guns, Explosives, Railroad Yards, Mothers, Fathers and on and on.

**

Others want us to be reduced to answering Yes or No, Good or Bad, Up or Down. "You have two choices," is a common ultimatum. Yet we have a multitude of choices and gradations within these selections. There are degrees in every "absolute". So were concocted Purgatory and Limbo; gray areas between Heaven and Hell. Shading the extremes of War and Peace, there are embargoes, blockades, spying, propaganda, confrontations, police actions, sabotage, and terrorism. Also, "Thou shalt not kill.": *except.... ..*

**

If you want to know what I think on any matter simply ask me. I will give an opinion. Subjective and even illogical as it may be, it will enlighten you as to what I think. From my answers you will derive insight; if not bearing directly upon the matter in question, then, at least, into the quality of my thinking.

**

The theory of evolution has so far been open to further examination. Theories are always in question. There is, for instance, no *theory* of gravity. There is a proven *law* of gravity. In science a theory becomes a law only when it has been subjected to testing by every means available. Religion is neither a theory nor a law. It is a *belief* or system of beliefs. One believes or disbelieves or is in doubt. Science deals in investigations. A laboratory is neither necessary nor sufficient to the test of a belief. Religion *assumes* absolutes and *decrees* laws.

**

If a boy lives a financially deprived life he works hard as a man to see that his son will have the best of everything. His son then lives well with little hard work. The young man has no respect for money and, as his own family begins to form, he loses job after job and squanders his legacy. Consequently his son is raised in relative poverty, promising himself to work hard so that *his* son will want for nothing. (The same cycles apply to paternal discipline and other matters). I call this theory The Alternation of Generations. This Alternation of Generations may be disrupted by the premature death of the father or the awareness by the father of the syndrome; either resulting, perhaps, in the breaking of the cycle. I speak from experience and observation. Yet I may be totally wrong. I have no degrees in psychology.

***

The avaricious man cares not about the poor or underprivileged. To him they are but the bodies over which he climbs to achieve his financial objective. That goal is ever-receding and is, simply stated, *more*.

***

If children were ever able to comprehend the depth of sacrifice made by their parents for the benefit of the young, they would avoid marriage as they would a herd of charging elephants. But children do not understand nor appreciate the burden of parenthood until it is upon them.

***

Scars of the body have painful causes yet most soon heal. Disfigurements of the psyche, though invisible, remain aching, open sores and are visible and repulsive only to the victim. They heal slowly, if ever.

***

Composer Marc Blitzstein: "Man has wanted to fly ever since the first time he tried and found that he couldn't". The fable of the fall of Icarus; his feathered wings, tallow and the hot sun, was told about three thousand years ago. Man retained the dream. His first powered flight occurred a short one hundred years ago. Now we send men to our Moon and two unmanned flights to Mars. We watch it all on television. The acceleration of man's knowledge is represented by these visually awesome events. Earth has switched to "fast forward".

***

Diversity is the secret of evolution and the survival of every species. Therefore do not expect agreement on every subject from any one person. Opinions differ. That is why the word "opinion" was devised. Be grateful if you have a friend or a mate with whom you can agree more than half of the time.

***

I hold very few beliefs: Freedom of Thought, Representational Government, Freedom of Religion, Rights of Privacy and the Power of Language.
Other convictions will have to seek residence elsewhere.

***

The babe survives by dint of love. The child thrives by the caring nature of
the society. The adolescent struggles in the company of his peers. The
youthful father and mother exist by the natural laws of mutual interdepend-
ence. Maturity consists of putting aside all lessons of the past and learning
to exist through the devices of social interaction and spiritual solitude.

***

Your beloved parents, your spouse, your children, your closest friends, your
own body will too soon be gone. There is no fit manner of preparation for
the inevitable. The only, paltry consolation; the first and last little hope is
resigned recognition of the facts. Then live fully this brief journey: from the
luck of your birth to the final, feeble tick of your heart. It is a good thing;
this life.

***

Allow for exceptions. A warrior may be thought of as violent by his nature.
A priest may seem Holy. A child is innocent. War is bad. Peace is good.
God is merciful. The weather is fine. All these beliefs are based on assump-
tions which may not apply in every case. Learn the words "except when". A
lazy, good-for-nothing loafer invented the arm chair upon which you now
rest your tired bones. An *absolute* is very hard to find.

***

The death of a child is properly seen as a universal tragedy. The little thing
had yet to achieve full blossom. There was only a beginning. There was no
middle and no proper ending. The whole society joins in the mourning. For
it is a universal axiom that all living things have a right to achieve maturity.
When such a statute is broken Nature herself weeps.

***

Adulthood arrives, like a stranded traveler at your door. It is prefaced not
by a knock but by the sudden realization that nothing lasts forever.

***

We are told that there is, in each of us, a genetic component which times
our bodies to grow, to mature and then to waste away into death. This
seems true of all plants and animals. It is also true of all societies and
governments. All living things march in time toward their own dissolution.

***

After many decades of trying and failing, I have learned to use the fly swatter. It was the process of trial and error that taught me and honed my skills. Just today I killed a small spider. I have been bitten by these more than once, and even though it is their nature to bite, it is my nature to kill that which bites me. I can't help it. The mortal blow was swift and can have caused almost no pain. My conscience is clear. He died bravely. I slew him not for what he did but for what he might have done. My conscience is clear.

***

Each pledge we fulfill is a step up the ladder of credibility. The failure to keep sacred even one promise sends the ladder crashing to the ground. Our honor lies there in a heap of kindling. Therefore be frugal with your pledges and honor those you undertake.

***

It may be embarrassing to have your dire predictions proved wrong. It is always a tragedy to see them proved right.

***

The death of a child is a universal tragedy. The death of an old man, surviving into his "second childhood", is not nearly so sad. The first is a shocking deprivation; the last is, to the dead, a welcome gift.

***

My parent's marriage may not have been made in Heaven. I was not made in Heaven. But I am trying like hell to get there.

***

After all these years, I find it most surprising that I am still able to be surprised. Yet another reason to live.

***

I will not join in a debate unless I can add facts. Otherwise I will listen to both sides so that I may learn. But when I hear an argument where logic is absent and tempers are hot, where each side desires only to win, I take a walk into the woods to relax. I listen to the wind and watch the wild critters.

***

The older one gets the more he should trust his instincts. His earlier, personal encounters and transactions, awkward situations, social blunders, etc., prepare him for the future. We all learn from personal history. Therefore keep a clear head and give rein to your intuition. Let your biography guide you.

***

I get my best ideas for stories when I am fresh awake in the morning. I often lie there polishing them in my mind, determined to write them down promptly after I rise, shower and shave. By the time I dress and walk to my writing table they are gone. How many wondrous, world shaping notions lie lost in the air, somewhere between my bed and my study?

***

It is strange that the writer dreads his literary critics while every day, close around him, are those who are happy to criticize his entire life.

***

In writing first drafts, I always overwrite. Actors in rehearsal often overact. Copy editors and stage directors find it easier to subtract than to add. They, like well-trained butchers, cut away the hide, the fat and the tripe to produce the essential, pleasing product within. I need an editor like a bull needs a butcher.

***

In the beginning there was a puzzle. Then you decided to solve the puzzle. Then you undertook to solve the puzzle. Then came the struggle, the labor, the extension of all your powers in the effort. At length came the solution. Once solved, the puzzle was no longer a puzzle. It had transformed into merely another fact to add to your collection. Somewhere during this process you were most excited, lost in the struggle, subservient to the problem and supremely blissful. Where, exactly, was that point? So you cast about, seeking another puzzle. It is the way of man.

***

A few decades ago it was fashionable, in some quarters, to test the theory that the differences between man and woman were learned rather than inherent. We were all a bit crazy then so the discussions may be forgiven. Yet these conversations were serious and sometimes lasted into the night, often ending in quarrels. While in the homes of every person with even a whit of education, rested, unopened, a dusty book of basic biology. And in the garden and the field; in the forest and the stream lay the obvious resolution.

I may be wrong but I am intellectually honest. When I am proved to be in error I admit it promptly and move ahead. Arguments are the signs of preparation for battle. They are mock wars. They are exercises fit only to train the uninitiated. The mature, battle tested intellectual moves quickly toward reconciliation, either by producing supportive facts, seeking arbitration, or simply evincing a surrender, (resorting, perhaps, to intellectual, guerrilla tactics). Pride, even in the face of logic or facts, will not allow the admission of error. Pride is the vice of the immature. Imbedded in religious belief and political persuasion is a passion where logic is impermissible. Never argue with a passion.

***

To survive in this world, we must learn to separate reality from fantasy. But the artist combines the two into a whole greater than the sum of its parts. Follow the artist as he bids us join him, romping in his wondrous world.

***

Often it takes an hour for me to write a paragraph. I may be a slow writer, a slow thinker or perhaps I have an obsessive personality; never satisfied. Or it may be that I think too much about the past, the present and the future; or about my goals in writing, or my readers or myself. I may have too many reference books or too ample a thesaurus or too short a memory which contains too many facts. Whatever it is, I wish I could write faster.

***

A father who teaches his children the precepts of charity is certain to find caring hands in attendance during his last days on this Earth.

***

I used to study to discover what it is that makes things funny but I gave up. It is too great a task. Today I merely concentrate on laughing.

***

Each of us has the soul of an explorer. Some of us are so intrepid as to risk the harrowing trek, deep into our own minds. There, an undiscovered landscape reveals angels and dragons, flying horses and impish elves and surprising, even shocking reflections of ourselves. Our minds hide hordes of fantastic ideas. Such expeditions of self-discovery require great courage.

***

Religious fanatics abounded in the Middle Ages. Their excesses are legendary. A few of their descendants survive today. When I hear one of them preach about the wrath of God, the tortures of the damned and the approach of Armageddon, I am angered to the point of blasphemy. I want to shout out, "What about love?" May God forgive me.

***

It was once said: "He who would conquer the entire world must first conquer his own mind". Now it may be proclaimed that it is enough to master, then control, all modern weaponry and be ready to use it.

***

Absolute fairness is an abstraction; a goal beyond realization. But let the strong become rational and insightful and they will perceive that the protection of the weak is essential to the survival of the mighty. Enlightened self-interest, practiced by the powerful, invariably fosters a high degree of fairness.

***

As a young boy, when confronted by conspicuous beauty in a woman, I grew weak. Today, in my declining years, my response is identical. But between then and now there was much pleasure, joy and mischief.

***

When one lives a long, full life, he can watch as certain sins of yesterday become today's virtues and history's heroes become exposed as fools.

***

Statues and monuments are often named for the brutal and ruthless tyrants who commissioned them. After the revolution these are quickly reconfigured. The sites are renamed in terms of the people.

***

And Man created God. It happened on the first day that man sought the answer to an important question and discovered that there was none.

***

We are well-taught to finish tasks which we start. Surely, it is the mark of responsibility to do so. Yet, as we did not begin our life, so we will not finish it. A series of events began and will conclude that adventure.

***

In every day of every productive life there are problems old and new. It is in the process of solving these problems that we find success, rewards and satisfaction. Take away the problems and we cease to be alive. Does not every bird, beast, fish, flower, snake and worm face hourly problems? Then who and what are we? We are the caretakers of a wild planet. Be grateful.

***

When the state executes a criminal it signals a failure. The criminal justice system has failed. Society has failed. We bury our mistakes.

***

Some men are uncomfortable in the company of many others. Some are loath to spend time alone. There is much to learn from both circumstances. Avoid neither but grow into ease and seek accomplishment in both.

***

In battle one army conquers another. In love the victors and vanquished are indistinguishable. The strong and the weak flow into each other as streams join into rivers; each party fully incorporating the other. In love, to lose is to win. Victory then rightly belongs to the society.

***

What we learn at home can be of benefit to us as we head out onto the street. The things one learns on the street may be useful in the home. One can learn to thrive in all circumstances. But leave the street out on the street.

***

I am mystified by the complexities of the piano. I watch masters play and find myself comparing their work to that of a master magician. They cause things to happen that I am certain are impossible. Yet they perform, not by dint of conjuring, but by the process of laborious study and practice. That is their secret. Indeed, those are the secrets of the master illusionist. I am mystified by the results of their dedication and toil.

***

No amount of education can teach a man to think. Learning originates outside the mind while thought occurs within.

***

It is the nature of education that the teacher be left behind. His best hope for a glimpse at immortality is to be remembered by his students. Yet he is happy to see the flame of knowledge pass from his lamp. There is always ample fuel remaining for the next class.

We may longingly anticipate retirement . Yet things are usually not as they appear; especially in our fantasies. We may become burdened with free time. Yet, with luck and proper planning, we will soon be busier than we ever were; joyfully self-employed by the most demanding boss we have ever endured: ourselves. Retire and become productive. Recreate yourself.

***

The most self-destructive emotion of man is bitterness. The most useless emotion; hatred. The most hateful; vengeance.

***

Every scientific breakthrough carries with it the destruction of one or two demigods. Often yesterday's sacred belief becomes today's irrelevant fable.

***

Modern Man is the only animal who so intrusively alters his environment to suit his desires. The rest intrude on their surroundings only to feed and to reproduce. These latter often fill their needs and adapt through migration or hibernation. Indigenous Man has responded in a similar way. Only modern Man survives through drastic alteration of the landscape. Adaptation and alteration struggle for primacy. Of all animals, only man can destroy Earth.

***

Of all the people to whom I owe gratitude and respect; (the soldier at the gate, the builder of my home, the teacher of my children), none looms higher than the person who prepares my food.

***

The banks of this river are high. They contain the rushing water every Spring. I am safe from flood. Yet the bloated city sprawls unabated with hungry mouth and concrete tentacles to engulf the countryside. The city pursues me wherever I go. It will hunt me down. It will consume me.

***

In Bowbells, North Dakota, the ice forms thick on the ponds by October 1st. Snow stays on the ground till mid-June. A child can freeze to death. In Bardstown, Kentucky, ice may not appear all year. When it does so, precocious children fall through and sometimes drown. In Ramrod Key, Florida, there is never any ice but there are alligators, snakes and an ocean filled with danger to threaten the unwary youngsters. Everywhere children are ever in danger.

***

To insulate oneself form all potential enemies is to isolate oneself from any and all would-be friends. The cynic is ever a reclusive, lonely man.

**

Marches, fanfares and battle themes are sounded with brass and drum. Churches preach to the music of the pipe organ. Strings and wind instruments paint landscapes. Only the guitar, in its many forms, plucked and strummed, is played with love for the sake of love.

**

The Ten Commandments are nine too many.
Our redemption requires but one.
"Be kind to one another." outrivals any.
Then submit to Him: "Thy will be done."

**

Religion and politics are not suited to light conversation. Neither should politics be a subject for the pulpit, nor religion advocated in the legislature.

**

I have known young men who would gladly engage in a battle to the death to gain the favors of a special woman. Yet to spend thousands of lives to gain salt, sugar, rubber, oil, or diamonds? This seems absurd to me. Who is there that will die for a diamond? Therefore leaders concoct fantasies to befuddle the populace and their armies. They tell us that these wars are about "self defense", "freedom" or "liberty". Then off we go. The ruse works every time.

**

Most wars are pointless. They ultimately bring shame upon both the generals and statesmen. They are merely fodder for historians and cannons alike.

**

There is an optimum time to eat the fruit of the tree. Too soon or too late and we loose the moment of perfect flavor. So ideas may arrive before the words to express them have been designed. Love can arrive too soon or too late. Perhaps I should have lived a hundred years ago or a century hence. We do the best we can with time. We settle for an approximation.

**

Most of the things we dread never occur. It is unexpected events that deserve our relentless, scrupulous attention. Prepare for the unexpected.

Lies are the very substance of all wars. Lies are the seeds planted in the minds of the pre-war populace, designed to make war acceptable. Lies then allow war to flourish and rising body counts to become acceptable as both sides pray to God for victory in their "just" endeavor. Yet the greatest lies are saved for the post war period. Honest historians commit lies of omission for lack of "classified" materials and decades later revisionist historians thrive on newly released *half truths*: lies of the most pernicious strain. Finally, when political leaders speak blatant lies to the populace, the decline of the nation becomes clearly visible upon the near horizon. The historians await their cue.

***

Courts may hear a hundred reasons for a crime but not one excuse.

***

The runner runs, he says, for exercise and relaxation; for pleasure. Running relaxes him. What was a thrice weekly jog is now a daily event. The distance increases weekly. He does not run to a place. He does not run because he is in a hurry nor to stay in good physical condition. He has become habituated to his body's natural endorphins. The run is a daily habit: a chemical dependency. The running is its own cause and its own objective. It is now the runner's dominant addiction. Make way for the runner. He runs high upon his path.

***

In my life I have known at least twenty women I would have gladly married and had a dozen reasons to marry each. Yet today I am happy that they got away. A single man has enough problems.

***

There is too much money in the business of war for it ever to be abolished. The same can be said of every other illegal, human vice.

***

The peacemakers are outnumbered. The soldiers are conditioned. The enemy is identified. The weapons are primed and the peace talks are adjourned. We now have allies that were lately our enemies as we declare war upon our former cobelligerents. The slaughter is at hand. Let the countdown begin.

***

A vice may be a sin but take care before declaring it a crime. To make of a vice a crime is to declare the Government the enforcer of the laws of the Church. Liberty allows me to make foolish choices. My weakness (if it harms no other), produces its own punishment. Has the historic, now fully discredited, Federal Prohibition of alcohol (1920-1933) taught us nothing?

***

We often hear the phrase, "Well, he means well,", as if to excuse some abhorrent act. Every dictator, tyrant, war monger and lynch mob "means well".

***

Someday, perhaps, peace talks will be convened to preempt a war.

***

We all want to live for a long time. But if longevity were the prime wish of man he would certainly worship the sequoia tree.

***

Our nation spends billions of dollars to protect us from our foreign enemies and not one cent is dedicated to seeking compromise; which is always the end game of war. Total victory is an illusion.

***

At Arlington Cemetery the warriors in the caskets are lowered by a machine. The bugler mourns with doleful melody. Seven rifles are sounded three times. The grass is wet with morning dew mixed with mourners' falling tears. The boy in the brown earth hears and sees nothing but he whispers to us of peace.

***

Your child is a gift to the world, assigned to you for care and tutelage. Do your duty and, though you be obscure, you will earn the praise of future generations.

***

The de-humanizing aspects of imprisonment begin with the prisoners. They soon spread to the correction officers and thence to their superiors. Eventually this lack of care spreads through the courts, the policing agencies and then throughout the general populace. Our society becomes merely a nation of convicts and jailers. Justice and Mercy are now merely words in The Bible.

***

We read the writings of others in the hope of discovering ourselves.

***

I had no idea of just how twisted human beings are until I read a work by Sigmund Freud, written in 1930, alerting me to the curruption of Man.

What with our inate agression and our repressed (or not) libido, our need to conquer and displace others of our species, it is a wonder that we ever slithered forth from the primordial muck. I guess it was just dumb luck.

***

No language can say it all. Often silence speaks our most profound thoughts.

***

Democracy is not a basic human need like hunger or reproduction. To flourish, it must be taught, practiced and fully understood. Like all beliefs, it must be nurtured from one generation to the next and protected against heretics who would pervert it to their own private purposes. So, from time to time, we fight to protect democracy in our homeland and we pray for democracy to thrive in all the world. We are missionaries for democracy, not armored, invading crusaders. One does not spread truth by killing non-believers.

***

All civil strife if fratricide. Yet this can be said of every war that ever was and every murder; starting with the first brothers in The Bible.

***

Mandatory, minimum sentences rob judges their ability to judge. Justice is blind but let the judges be ever wise and vigilant lest the system become computerized and honorable, judicious jurists become antique.

***

The mythological Narcissus, rejecting others, fell into love with his own image as reflected in the surface of a pool. A self-absorbed body worshiper poses for pictures and preens in front of a glass mirror. Know that all flesh putrefies. The body is but one aspect of life. Enlightened action awaits the effective man.

***

Show me a man with boundless hunger for money and a "tunnel vision" and I will show you a budding miser. This man will never have "enough" money and never learn how to use it. His last act in life will be to count his pocket change.

***

I know of no monogamous mammal. Only Man pretends to be so. Why?

***

Slaves are always kept ignorant of every aspect of life to which they are not specifically assigned. Reading is often prohibited. In this way they are restrained from aspiring to a loftier status. So the freed workers of today, the providers of "heavy lifting", are generally deprived of the extensive education required to improve their lot. An ignorant class of people is required in order to maintain the status quo. Perhaps their children will be afforded learning.

***

Temptation must be either avoided altogether or immediately embraced. Either way there will certainly be regret. Be it by a bowl of fancy cookies or a handsome, yielding lady, we are tested every day.

***

There is a two-toed sloth that lives only in Panama. There is a blue-green algae which grows only within the fur of this species of sloth. There is a mite which subsists solely upon the algae that grows within the fur of this two-toed sloth in Panama. What are we to think?

***

To be unafraid in battle is to be insane. To be fearful yet to persevere is to be brave. To begin a war is criminal. To search for peace; heroic.

***

Beware of routine. The man who travels the same path every day will never see anything new. He soon rejects all the unfamiliar; resents all change. He lives in yesterday. It were better for him that he had been made a boulder.

***

Of all the roles the actor ever plays, the most challenging depiction is of himself. He discovers Hamlet or Stanly Kowalsky with practiced ease, yet can become lost in the search for his own identity.

***

Those who tempt are guilty of sin. Those who yield are guilty of vulnerability. In The Bible it is The Devil who tempts and God who has the power to forgive. God has never tempted anyone.

***

We civilians may forget the war fought long ago, but what of the veteran? He does not forget. He lies there with but one leg and one eye; lies on the edge of oblivion. Every morning when he awakes, he remembers the war but forgets its causes. He did his duty.

***

The neighborhood youngsters are too loud. Their blasting music pounds my ears and strips away all thinking. I plot to destroy their sound equipment. I lay a curse upon their ears. Yet I hesitate. The party will end before dawn. Silence will return. Now is the time for me to pay for the sins of my youth.

***

A revolution is kin to a sacrament of purification. In its aftermath, on some still fertile ground, lie the seeds of another such sacred, ritual upheaval.

***

What would I give to be with her for only one hour? All my treasure. But even one year would not be long enough. I am shamelessly thirsty for my lost love.

***

No nation has the right nor the power to alter the religious beliefs of another. Even the mighty, yet tormented Pontius Pilate understood this.

***

If you would avoid a brutal thrashing, never utter one derogatory word to a man about his wife, his horse or his dog.

***

The General's task is to end the war and thus render himself redundant. He may become a tirelessly enthusiastic peacemaker; a favorite of the gods. In a war-torn, weary world the peacemaker is a saint.

***

Man is a reasoning creature. He will successfully apply his most diligent efforts in solving the most difficult problem and then be rendered foolish by the smile of a lovely woman. Man has his limits; beyond which is Woman.

***

Those who never dream are convinced that dreams never come true. Those who now fly to the Moon and beyond ride on the fantasies of Icarus. Man has the ability to fashion reality from the cloth of his dreams.

***

When good news calls at the front door, don't answer the knock at the back.

***

I see that very few women are arrested each year for robbery, burglary, smuggling or rape. In general, women are well behaved. However they do murder their husbands from time to time. This I do not understand.

***

Advances in DNA research have caused many innocent convicts to be released. Others, guilty ones, have been rightly incarcerated. The prisons remain full but the courts are more just. Laws of science help balance the scales of justice.

***

The faster the treadmill the faster you run; the sooner you tire. You are going nowhere. Get off. Move at your own pace, straight toward your own star.

***

Of all the beautiful rings she had ever owned; had ever been gifted, she remembered with most clarity and fondness the one made from a dandelion stem, given to her by lost Billy, when she was but nine years old.

***

It may be too late to correct mistakes of omission or commission made with your children. If you are lucky, you may have another chance; by nurturing and fostering theirs.

***

More men have been slaughtered in battles "of honor" than have died in wars of liberation. For the honor of a nation its leaders are willing to sacrifice its richest treasure: the lives of its faithful, young soldiers. The dead never complain.

***

DROPS OF WATER, GRAINS OF SAND

When, as a child, I needed scolding, Mother dispensed it in a manner which never made me doubt her love. Yet I feared my father's wrath. So, praise from Mother was often discounted, while applause from Father was a golden crown. My sisters experienced the opposite reactions.

***

The publisher has my book. Will it ever see daylight? My lady has my letter of proposal. How will she respond? I will know the answers. Yet these days seem so long. Are they truly but twenty-four hours? I think not.

***

We all die, sooner or later: The later it is, the sooner we die. I have fought a few rounds with the Reaper and come away badly bruised. I am tired. There are but one or two rounds left. My only hope is that He dies before I do.

***

There is a nobility in certain breeds of dog that reminds one of The Saints. They have an unwavering sense of duty to the task assigned to them and a blind, unquestioning devotion to their Master. To own such a dog one must first be worthy. For, after all, you are his god.

***

Encouragement. It costs nothing to bestow, yet is an invaluable gift to the recipient. If you believe in a friend and his objective then cheer him on. Sports fans know this and so does every player. The artist is ever in need.

***

The babe in arms has a god complex. He first demands that the world conform to his every wish. The food, diapers and lullaby comprise his wants and needs and he receives them on demand. See how his parents learn to speak and understand his language? See how they sing and whisper and coo to him? See how they love him simply because he exists? Lucky baby. This is a god who must, over time, learn to become simply a man. And each man and woman will temporarily become proud slaves to their children.

***

From the beginning, the moment of the "Big Bang", to the final collapse of the Universe, there will be only one you; only one "I". The thought is certainly thrilling and even wonderful, yet intimidating. It puts a heavy burden upon each of us. What to do with this one life? How best to utilize this one shot at existence?. It is not an easy question to answer nor an easy quest once chosen. There is always the "What if" and the "I wish" to be considered and the "I regret" to be overcome. We often find relief from these constant, tormenting whispers by accepting "duty" and, as loyal children, loving parents and responsible citizens, we set aside our own dreams and desires waiting for that someday when we may attend to the needs of our own nature. To many that day never comes. To others it may come only when it seems "too late". Submission to the demands of society is a hard habit to break. To most happy people the awareness of duty to one's self came early and every other obligation became secondary. There is in them, and hiding in us, a mighty, inner core.

So we, not yet heroes but on the rising path, care for our loved ones: because *we want to*. We are loyal and loving to our spouses because that suits our purpose and need. We are faithful to friends because we value them and value friendship. We slowly learn to rank ourselves above all else and then, when we give of ourselves, it is indeed a great gift. When confronted with adversity we see mere obstacles, simply to be overcome. We do not slavishly tow the world nor are we grudgingly dragged along behind it. We ride it like a chariot and the reins are in our hands. By choosing early on to be the master of our life we do our duty, not because it is our duty but because it is our choice. When our chosen, *self-imposed*, obligations are fulfilled it is then quite easy for us to continue this pattern. We choose to fulfill all the potentialities we have so carefully cultivated and we gleefully grasp for the future. Having long ago conquered our inner selves we eagerly seek confrontation with that portion of the outer world which we desire. We succeed because we have acquired the *habit* of success. We have been preparing for future challenges and we greet them; embrace them as life-long companions. We succeed because it is, by now, *our nature* to succeed. And Death? Let it come in its time as it does to us all; even to The Universe.

The temperature is moderate. A light breeze cools me and animates every leaf out there. Each tree vies with its neighbor for the sun. There is enough sun for all. Each bird acts out his scripted role. Each insect bustles about the business of living. Every native animal I have come to admire is here this morning, in my yard, performing all the wonderful antics peculiar to its species. In all this tumult there is a sublimity. Chaos and order become indistinguishable. It is Sunday morning. My neighbors have gone, each to his place of devotion, while I sit here, at my window, devoutly worshipping at mine.

***

It seems strange to me that my advancing age has not generated a greater belief in an afterlife. Nor do I think of God, nor punishment, nor reward, as my father and his friends did in those last years of their lives. I know I should but I just don't. I will not mind if I simply turn to dust. If I meet the guard at the Gate or the Boatman at the River Styx, I am willing to be tested and, if found wanting, prepared for whatever is to come. I have never feared justice nor begged for mercy. I am the thing that sprung from the garden that was my childhood and my home. I am the product of my past. I have always been impelled by my own yesterday and I tried my best , though not always successfully, to shape my tomorrow toward virtue. I will be glad to have others weigh my sins against my positive deeds, for I cannot; will not judge myself. Perhaps there is another life after this. If so, then, as Peter Pan remarked, "To die will be an awfully big adventure!" (J.M. Barrie)

***

> I sent my soul through the Invisible,
> Some letter of that After-life to spell:
> And bye and bye my soul returned and answered,
> "Behold, I myself am Heaven and Hell"
> (Omahr Khayyam)

***

ISBN 141201699-1

9 781412 016995